A Quaker Goes to War

The Diary of
William Harvey Walter
Company F, 188th Pennsylvania Volunteers

William Harvey Walter, age 94

Transcribed and Edited by
Carol-Lynn Sappé

HERITAGE BOOKS
2008

HERITAGE BOOKS
AN IMPRINT OF HERITAGE BOOKS, INC.

Books, CDs, and more—Worldwide

For our listing of thousands of titles see our website
at
www.HeritageBooks.com

Published 2008 by
HERITAGE BOOKS, INC.
Publishing Division
100 Railroad Ave. #104
Westminster, Maryland 21157

Copyright © 2008 Carol-Lynn Sappé

All rights reserved. No part of this book may be reproduced or transmitted in any form or by any means, electronic or mechanical, including photocopying, recording or by any information storage and retrieval system without written permission from the author, except for the inclusion of brief quotations in a review.

International Standard Book Numbers
Paperbound: 978-0-7884-4636-8
Clothbound: 978-0-7884-7252-7

William Harvey Walter
Diary
1864

Transcribed and Edited
by
Carol-Lynn Sappé

For Richard,
with love

and to the memory of
William Harvey Walter
and all the men of
Company F,
188th Pennsylvania Volunteers

Table of Contents

List of Illustrations and Maps _____ ix

Foreword _____ xi

A Quaker Goes to War _____ xiii

About the Diary _____ xv

January 1864 _____ 7

February 1864 _____ 13

March 1864 _____ 19

April 1864 _____ 25

May 1864 _____ 31

June 1864 _____ 37

July 1864 _____ 43

August 1864 _____ 49

September 1864 _____ 55

October 1864 _____ 61

November 1864 _____ 67

December 1864 _____ 73

Memoranda _____ 79

Cash Account January _____ 81

Cash Account February _____ 83

Cash Account March _____ 85

Cash Account April _____ 87

Cash Account May _____ 89

Cash Account June, July, August _____ 91

Cash Account September _____ 93

Cash Account October _____ 95

Cash Account November _____ 97

Cash Account December _____ 99

Summary of Accounts _____ 101

Memoranda _____ 103

The 188th Pennsylvania Volunteers	105
From the Book by Samuel P. Bates	111
Members of Company F	117
William Harvey Walter, Civilian Again	123
"Last Call Men"	125
The Harvey / Walter Family	127
G. D. Vanderveer	129
Maps	131
Photographs	137
Bibliography	143
Glossary of Names	145
Footnotes	153

List of Illustrations and Maps

p. i   William Harvey Walter, age 93 in 1935

p. xv   William Harvey Walter's Obituary

p. 3   Diary cover

p. 5   1864 calendar

p. 121   Ribbon worn by GAR Post Commanders

p. 127   Map of Fort Monroe and surrounding area

p. 127   Map of James River showing locations of Company F from embarkation on May 4 – 6, 1864

p. 128   Map of Richmond to Petersburg showing locations of Company F from May 7 – December 31, 1864

p. 129   Map of Petersburg, close-ups, showing location of 18th Corps June 15 – August 26, 1864

p. 130   Map of Petersburg, close-up, showing location of batteries June 15 – August 26, 1864

p. 130   Map of Drewry's Bluff to Deep Bottom including Chaffin's Farm 1864

p. 131   Map of Defensive Lines 18th Army Corps from Fort Brady to Fort Burnham (Battery Harrison)

p. 133   188th Pennsylvania Volunteers Infantry Banner

p. 133   The Lincoln Gun, Fortress Monroe, Virginia

p. 134   Captain of the Port's office and Hygeia Dining Saloon, Fortress Monroe, Virginia

p. 134   City Point, Virginia with boats on the James River

p. 135   An unidentified fortification at Petersburg

p. 135   Pontoon bridge across the Appomattox River

p. 136   Soldiers await transportation to medical help

p. 136   Hospital tents at City Point, Virginia

p. 136   Three surgeons of the 9th Corps hospital

p. 137   Fort Burnham / Harrison

p. 137   General Charles Jackson Paine

p. 137   Chesapeake Hospital, Fortress Monroe, VA

p. 137   Union 18th Corps badge

p. 137   GAR members' lapel pin

x

Foreword

I remember my great grandfather's diary lying on my mother's desk. She kept it there, a prized possession. What I most cherished, a hand colored portrait of my great grandfather in his Union uniform. It hung on the wall in my bedroom.

When William's daughter, my grandmother, passed away the portrait was given to my mother's younger sister. She had no right to it, the portrait hung in my room. I thought it my own. I remember crying till I fell into an exhausted sleep. I was six.

Adults seldom notice hurt feelings of a child but my mother understood. She told me my great grandfather's words had a far greater value than his portrait and to honor his memory I should keep his diary safe. And so I have through my many moves around the world. The small leather bound diary has always sat on my desk too.

One day in 2005 I noticed the book was looking tired. It was dusted regularly but now a page peeked out and the binding had a crack where none had been before. Opening the book carefully I realized the once vivid words written in pencil and ink were fading. At that moment it became clear, to honor William Harvey Walter's memory I would have to transcribe his words. And so it began.

The names in the diary piqued my curiosity. I began research to put a "face" to the names. One name in particular, William C. Horn, set me to work in earnest. My great grandfather had witnessed an act that would right a wrong.

William C. Horn, Company A of the 188th Pennsylvania Volunteers is listed in official records as a deserter. But, William Horn did not desert; he fell overboard and drowned while being transported to the front on
May 5, 1864, and my great grandfather was an eyewitness.

The consequences of deserting were far reaching, emotionally and financially. Horn's family suffered not knowing his fate. So to his memory, this book can set William C. Horn free, liberated of the charge of desertion and released to regain a place of honor in his family's memory.

The journey has freed me as well. Family research has shown from what stock my mother came.

I hope my many cousins and their children will one day read the words their great grandfather, great-great-grandfather and so on wrote. To honor his memory is worth more than a portrait.

Carol-Lynn Sappé

A Quaker Goes to War

A Quaker goes to war? A conundrum.

The Society of Friends (Quakers) follows the teachings of George Fox (1624 – 1691), an English nonconformist religious reformer.

Members of the society referred to themselves as Friends of Truth taken from John 15:15. The name Quakers derived from an encounter with a sarcastic English judge whom George Fox had admonished with the words: *"tremble at the word of the Lord."* The judge referred to Fox as a *"Quaker"* for the remainder of the trial and the term stuck. But, who was this "Quaker"?

A pious young man, George Fox questioned the church leaders of his time, looking for the one true religion. Becoming disenchanted with existing Christian institutions Fox at the age of twenty-three heard a voice from within speak *"there is one, even Christ Jesus, who can speak to thy condition"*. It was his call from God to go forth and preach the concept of the *Inward Light (Voice)*. The *"seed of Christ"* lay within everyone, to understand and comprehend the Word of God and to convey judgment on spiritual matters. An unorthodox view at that time and calls for his arrest and confinement followed him and those who converted to that belief.

The tenets of the belief:

• that every man and woman has direct access to God; no priestly class or "steeple houses" (churches) are needed

• that every person, male or female, slave or free is of equal worth

• that there is no need in one's religious life for elaborate ceremonies, rituals, gowns, creeds, dogma, or other "empty forms".

• following the inward light leads to spiritual development and towards individual perfection.

Further beliefs brought the society into direct conflict with Cromwell's Puritan government and later the restored monarchy of Charles II. They were:

• the refusal to pay tithes to the state church

• the refusal to take an oath in court

• the refusal to bear arms in time of peace or war

To underscore the refusal to bear arms in time of peace or war George Fox wrote the peace testimony in 1660:

"We utterly deny all outward wars and strife and fighting with outward weapons for any end or under any pretence whatever; this is our testimony to the whole world." George Fox, *A Declaration to the King*.

With the colonization of the New World many Friends left England hoping to avoid further harassment. In North America, however, the persecution of Quakers continued, especially in the Puritan colonies. With the establishment of Pennsylvania in 1682 by a Quaker, William Penn, religious tolerance became the common thread that bound the people of the Penn's Woods colony together. That is, until the Revolutionary War.

Quakers followed the tenet of remaining neutral even as the tension mounted between the colonies and the crown. When war broke out members refused to pay military taxes or to serve in the army. Tensions grew with their non-Quaker neighbors and many were driven off their land, their millstones ordered smashed and their homes burned. Many were arrested and forced into camps in Virginia.

After the Revolutionary War those who remained rebuilt their lives and hoped for continued peace. Yet by the War of 1812 the new states began to rely upon laws compelling their citizens to be part time soldiers in order to fight off the new British threat.

With the stirring of a war of brother against brother the pull between belief and patriotism was felt all across the Quaker community. The Monthly Meeting minutes of the time reaffirmed the peace testimony and reaction to member's abandonment of the rule varied from denunciation to silence.

"Quakers were by no means united on how to interpret the peace testimony or on how to put it into practice." John M. Moore, editor, *Friends in the Delaware Valley. Philadelphia Yearly Meeting 1681-1981.*

Samuel Harper stated, " ... the war troubled consciences here, as powerful roots of Quaker pacifism tugged one way and patriotism and hatred of slavery pulled another." Douglas R. Harper, *If Thee Must Fight: A Civil War History of Chester County, Pennsylvania.*

It was General Robert E. Lee's invasion of Pennsylvania in 1863 that finally turned the tide for many Quaker families.

"But since Lee's army has been massed in Pennsylvania, a change has come over our people, all seem to realize that, at last the magnitude of the threatening danger, and every one expresses his willingness to help drive the invader from the soil." The Invasion- The Response of Chester County- Scenes and incidents in West Chester in *Village Record* (July 7, 1863).

And so it was this atmosphere that allowed William Harvey Walter and his brother Townsend to enlist in the Union army.

About the Diary

Following are the words William H. Walter wrote in his diary in 1864. He was twenty-one years old at the beginning of 1864 and a soldier in the Union Army.

The diary was given to my mother by her grandfather William at the time of her marriage on June 20th, 1936. He called it his most prized possession and thought it made a fitting wedding gift. He also gave her a pair of earrings he had made out of buttons from his uniform. These earrings along with the diary remain prized possessions till this day.

The following obituary appeared in the Philadelphia newspaper after his death on Oct. 20th, 1936:

As members of the Society of Friends, the Walter family remembered the abuse and rebuff shown them during the Revolutionary War. The Walter men were millers and as stated previously, the family millstones as well as others were ordered smashed and their mills burned during the Revolutionary War and again during the War of 1812. In 1863 William's father John owned a mill at Christiana Hundred, Delaware, just across the Pennsylvania line. John and his second wife Elizabeth had young children to care for and the loss of the mill would put the family in peril. It was agreed that William, along with his brother Townsend H. Walter would enter service but not to bear arms, a promise that as time would tell was impossible to keep.

On November 30th, 1863, William enlisted at Media, Pennsylvania in Delaware County. He was given the rank of Private. On December 1st, 1863 he was promoted to Corporal when it was learned he could read and write. That same day, his younger brother Townsend joined Nield's Independent Battery, Delaware Light Artillery in Wilmington, Delaware, also at the rank of Private.[1]

Both Townsend and William were living in the state of Delaware at the time of their enlistment. Townsend was living at home with his father and stepmother at Christiana Hundred. William was boarding in Wilmington, Delaware.

After reading the diary and researching family history it became clear that William chose to enlist in Delaware County because of family ties and due to Delaware County offering a sizable bounty for enlisting.[2]

Having enlisted, both young men returned home to settle their accounts and prepare themselves for service.

The diary, transcribed here, was presented to William at Christmas, 1863 by his cousin Mary E. Hollingsworth.

Written in both pencil and ink, the diary contains notes, cash accounts, and entries. On two dates (December 1st and 2nd, 1864) code was substituted for words. The code is preserved in this edition. To this date it has not been deciphered.

The diary does not end with December 31st, 1864 as William continued to make daily entries through January 1865 and then sporadic entries up to December 18th, 1865. Entries were also made in 1866 and 1887 after William returned home. These entries are interesting as it showed the struggles that some soldiers met on entering the workforce upon leaving service.

William writes in thoughts. His words have been edited only where necessary for easier reading. His capitalization and syntax have been preserved. For clarity added words are shown in parenthesis.

Although many entries may seem mundane William found himself in the thick of combat: Swift Creek, Proctor's Creek, Drewry's Bluff, the Bermuda Hundred campaign, Cold Harbor, Hare's Hill, the siege of Petersburg, the assault of Fort Harrison, the battle of Chaffin's Farm, the battle of Fair Oaks, duty in the trenches before Richmond and occupation of Richmond and guard and provost duty at Lynchburg and in Central Virginia until December, 1865.

When the 188th Pennsylvania Volunteers mustered out at City Point, Va., December 14, 1865 the regiment had lost: 10 officers and 114 enlisted men killed in action, 2 officers and 66 enlisted men to disease. A total of 192 men lost.

Several maps have been added to aid the reader in following Company F's movements and those of William Harvey Walter in particular, along with footnotes, pictures and glossary of names. The *"History of Pennsylvania Volunteers 188th Regiment"* by Samuel P. Bates, prepared in compliance with acts of the Pennsylvania legislature is also present, as well as a complete roster of Company F.

It is hoped William's diary will aid research into Company F of the 188th Pennsylvania Volunteers.

Diary
1864

Presented to Wm. H. Walter by his cousin M. E. Hollingsworth
Dec. 25th, 1863

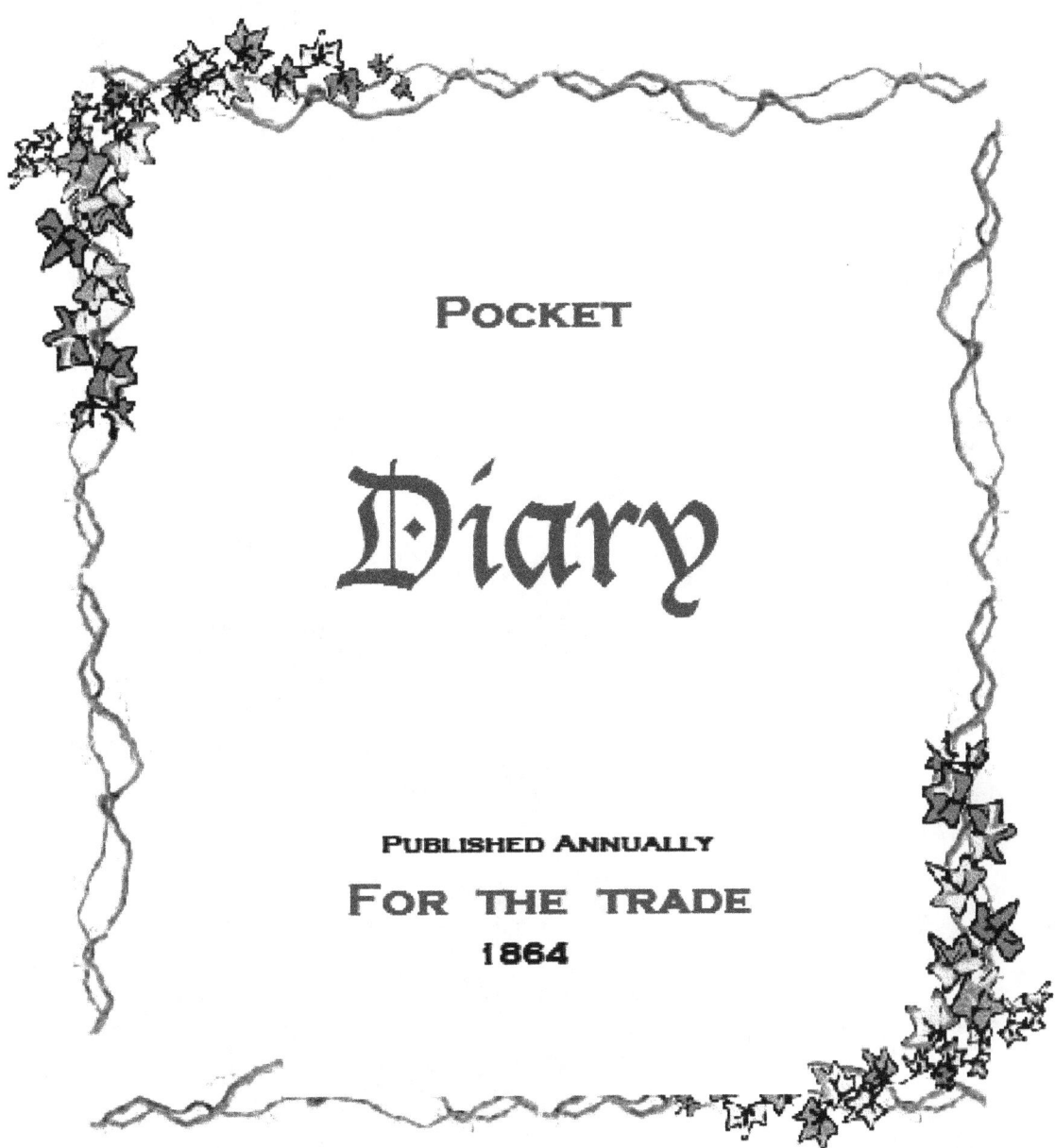

Pocket Diary

Published Annually For the Trade
1864

1864

January
S	M	T	W	T	F	S
					1	2
3	4	5	6	7	8	9
10	11	12	13	14	15	16
17	18	19	20	21	22	23
24	25	26	27	28	29	30
31						

February
S	M	T	W	T	F	S
	1	2	3	4	5	6
7	8	9	10	11	12	13
14	15	16	17	18	19	20
21	22	23	24	25	26	27
28	29					

March
S	M	T	W	T	F	S
		1	2	3	4	5
6	7	8	9	10	11	12
13	14	15	16	17	18	19
20	21	22	23	24	25	26
27	28	29	30	31		

April
S	M	T	W	T	F	S
					1	2
3	4	5	6	7	8	9
10	11	12	13	14	15	16
17	18	19	20	21	22	23
24	25	26	27	28	29	30

May
S	M	T	W	T	F	S
1	2	3	4	5	6	7
8	9	10	11	12	13	14
15	16	17	18	19	20	21
22	23	24	25	26	27	28
29	30	31				

June
S	M	T	W	T	F	S
			1	2	3	4
5	6	7	8	9	10	11
12	13	14	15	16	17	18
19	20	21	22	23	24	25
26	27	28	29	30		

July
S	M	T	W	T	F	S
					1	2
3	4	5	6	7	8	9
10	11	12	13	14	15	16
17	18	19	20	21	22	23
24	25	26	27	28	29	30
31						

August
S	M	T	W	T	F	S
	1	2	3	4	5	6
7	8	9	10	11	12	13
14	15	16	17	18	19	20
21	22	23	24	25	26	27
28	29	30	31			

September
S	M	T	W	T	F	S
				1	2	3
4	5	6	7	8	9	10
11	12	13	14	15	16	17
18	19	20	21	22	23	24
25	26	27	28	29	30	

October
S	M	T	W	T	F	S
						1
2	3	4	5	6	7	8
9	10	11	12	13	14	15
16	17	18	19	20	21	22
23	24	25	26	27	28	29
30	31					

November
S	M	T	W	T	F	S
		1	2	3	4	5
6	7	8	9	10	11	12
13	14	15	16	17	18	19
20	21	22	23	24	25	26
27	28	29	30			

December
S	M	T	W	T	F	S
				1	2	3
4	5	6	7	8	9	10
11	12	13	14	15	16	17
18	19	20	21	22	23	24
25	26	27	28	29	30	31

January 1864

Friday, January 1st, 1864
> Left Baltimore, 5 o'clock PM, where we arrived night-before, for Fortress Monroe[3] with 37 men, 2 of whom Deserted in Baltimore prior to starting. Casey & Smith.

Saturday, January 2nd, 1864
> Spent this Day in fixing our tent. My companions are D. Etter, A. Robertson, & F. Haslehurst. Not quite so cold as it was yesterday.

Sunday, January 3rd, 1864
> Sun came out since and company had inspection of knapsacks and accoutrements at 9 o'clock. Field parade at 3 o'clock with the Band playing.

Monday, January 4th, 1864
> Still the usual routine of drill which we have to do now twice a day, 1-½ hours each time. The Regiment had another dress parade.

Tuesday, January 5th, 1864
> Nice and warm. Sun shining Brightly. There was some Co(mpany) orders read to us from the Captain. To Raising the colors.

Wednesday, January 6th, 1864
> Colder than it was. Battalion Drill by the whole Regiment. Exercised us Recruits. Was no Dress parade this evening.

Thursday, January 7th, 1864
> Drilling again twice today. Started to snow and Blow in the evening and continued all night without intermission.

Friday, January 8th, 1864
> This morning there was quite a lot of snow on the ground and very cold and disagreeable. Had no Drill on account of it.

Saturday, January 9th, 1864
> Had no Drill this Day of account of the snow. Still cold and disagreeable. Drew the set of my uniform, dress hat, coat, blouse, pants, Canteen & shoes.

Sunday, January 10th, 1864
> Sun came out, clear. We had inspection of knapsacks this morning. Had dress parade in the evening with Band playing. J. Rush & J. Burns came while (I was) out.

Monday, January 11th, 1864
> Sun came out warm and the snow melting now fast. I was very wet while drilling. A. Robertson and myself was on Kitchen Police carrying water and washing dishes.

Tuesday, January 12th, 1864
> Received a letter from Father. While eating dinner the sentence of a Prisoner was read out on Dress parade to be shot to death for Desertion.

Wednesday, January 13th, 1864
> Did not Drill today, was employed in moving our tents which took all Day. There was a slight fall of rain in the afternoon which prevented Dress Parade.

Thursday, January 14th, 1864
: Drilled twice today. Weather still keeps wet and cloudy. Wrote and mailed a letter to Mary Velotte this afternoon.

Friday, January 15th, 1864
: Weather quite warm and cloudy. Drilled this afternoon with light artillery pieces.

Saturday, January 16th, 1864
: The weather is nice warm & clear. Snow all gone today. Was chosen (to) Police cleanup all around. Received a letter from Father.

Sunday, January 17th, 1864
: Had the usual inspection of arms, knapsack and accoutrements this morning. Received a letter from Kate S. Dedin. Still weather warm and clear. Sixty fine new recruits arrived.

Monday, January 18th, 1864
: Cloudy and warm and towards noon starting to rain. Continued all afternoon and night. Received a letter from Bro. Joe[4] containing picture of my tent.

Tuesday, January 19th, 1864
: Cleared off at noon and blowed up cold. Drilled with light field pieces in the afternoon. Filled our beds with Hay for the first time.

Wednesday, January 20th, 1864
: Little warmer then it was. Sun shining brightly. Wrote a letter to Rosie in the afternoon. Drilled at the guns again in the afternoon.

Thursday, January 21st, 1864
: Received a box from home containing Pies, cakes, apples and Sugar & c. Also received a letter from Phebe A. Sharpless. On Nit then Police with Robertson.

Friday, January 22nd, 1864
: Was drilling on the water Battery this forenoon and firing Blank cartridge. Wrote a letter home and one to Phebe Anna. This afternoon Andy Blair was released from the Guardhouse.

Saturday January 23rd, 1864
: This day as all Saturdays was employed in Policing up. Wrote a letter to Kate S. Dedin in the afternoon. The day was quite warm.

Sunday, January 24th, 1864
: Most splendid weather. Obtained a pass and went out and had a stroll up the beach. Received a letter from Rosie and Brother Townsend who has embarked for N. Orleans.

Monday, January 25th, 1864
: Quite warm all Day. Received a letter from Cousin M.E. Hollingsworth in answer to mine. The First Class Drilled. My Company Drilled as per Order.

Tuesday, January 26th, 1864
: Weather continued to be warm and was quite hot while drilling. Wrote s letter to Rosie in the afternoon and also to Parson Brownlow.[5]

Wednesday, January 27th, 1864
> Still continued to be hot. Nothing happened of any interest today. We drilled at the field. Police now all together in the afternoon.

Thursday, January 28th, 1864
> Hotter then ever today. To hot to stay in the tent. Wrote a letter to J.D. Velotte this Evening.

Friday, January 29th, 1864
> Still as hot as ever (this) A.M. Was firing mortar Practice today from the North East front of the Rampart of the Fort. Got a hat made for Sunday articles.

Saturday, January 30, 1864
> Was an exciting Day. Besides heavy Cannonading the Matthew Hospital[6] took fire and one ward was burned. Our company was called out and we ran 2 miles but was to late.

Sunday, January 31st, 1864
> Gloomy and dull all Day. Cannonading still continues today. Received a letter from Mary Velotte and answered it in the afternoon and also wrote one Home.

February 1864

Monday, February 1st, 1864
> Raining this forenoon but stopped in time for Drill. An English Man of War came in the harbor and fired a Salute which was returned by the Main Batteries of the Fort.

Tuesday, February 2nd, 1864
> Received a letter from Kate S. Dedin and wrote one to Dr. Vernon about getting the "Delaware County"[7]. Sergeant G. Roberts and Corporal Davis returned.

Wednesday, February 3rd, 1864
> Raining all night and most of the morning. Cleared off at 10 o'clock. Returned all our old Guns in and received New ones instead. 150 New Recruits came this morning.

Thursday, February 4th, 1864
> Cleared off. Clear and cold. Drilled in the manual of Arms by the Captain with our new Guns in the afternoon. Company H of our Regiment left camp for service on Gun Boats.

Friday, February 5th, 1864
> Received three letters, one from Naomi, one from Isaac Johnson and the other from E. Normall. Also received the Delaware Paper that I subscribed for sometime ago. Wrote a letter to Kate Dedin.

Saturday, February 6th, 1864
> Obtained pass and went out of the Fort. Returned before Noon and wrote two letters. One to E. Normall and the other to Father.

Sunday, February 7th, 1864
> Rather warm and it has been for a few Days. Laid in my tent all Day reading a Book called "Wild Western Series".

Monday, February 8th, 1864
> On Kitchen Police with Williamson.

Tuesday, February 9th, 1864
> Haselhurst and Robertson on Kitchen Police. In the evening went down to Company D to see Harry Hale and D. Ball. Came back and wrote to Miss Mary Ellwood a short note.

Wednesday, February 10th, 1864
> Weather, nice and clear but the wind cold. Wrote a letter to Isaac Johnson in the afternoon in answer to his. Feeling unwell.

Thursday, February 11th, 1864
> Went to the Doctor this morning but no pass. Was on Duty. Had to stop in the midst of Drill and vomit. Wrote a letter to Isaac Johnson in the evening. Cold nights with wind.

Friday, February 12th, 1864
> Obtained a pass and went out of the Fort. Did not drill today's Company Parade. Got my Dress coat fixed and appeared on Dress parade for the first time since I was here.

Saturday, February 13th, 1864
> Went out along with 1 other of the recruits for Police but was ordered back by the Adjutant to Drill but though I would not have to so I left until Drill was over.

Sunday, February 14th, 1864
> After inspection this morning the Recruits were called in to line and drilled to see who was fitted to enter the old company. Myself and 20 others were selected.[8]

Monday, February 15th, 1864
> Drilled with the old company on the Ramparts with no Ordinance. Continued raining at 1 and continued all Day and Night. Was detailed for Guard tomorrow.

Tuesday, February 16th, 1864
> Mounted Guard this morning for the first time with Knapsack. To Picket and Guard at Oniel Oak Bridge.[9] Blowed up cold afternoon. Coldest weather this winter.

Wednesday, February 17th, 1864
> Came off Guard at ½ past 5 o'clock. Wind blew hard all Day. D. Etter mounted guard also this morning for the first time.

Thursday, February 18th, 1864
> Wind abated somewhere towards Night. Drilled only once today on account of the cold. More New Recruits arrived to Day.

Friday, February 19th, 1864
> Still continues to be as cold if not colder that it has been this winter. So cold we did not Drill at all to Day. Changed my tent and went in with A. McMichael, J.H. Palmer & Geo. Blain.

Saturday, February 20th, 1864
> A little milder then it has been for a few days. Was occupied all Day in Policing and cleaning up. Five New Corporals made to Day.

Sunday, February 21st, 1864
> Had the usual inspection and the articles of war read to us. Nothing of interest transpired. Received another issue of the Delaware Co. Paper.

Monday, February 22nd, 1864
> Went on Guard this morning. Had Post No. 11. An interesting Guard at the Magazine. A Salute was fired and a general celebration by the Company and Regiment. Washington's Birth Day.

Tuesday, February 23rd, 1864
> Came off Guard this morning at 10 o'clock. Cleaned up my Kit and went outside after dinner and came in about 2 o'clock.

Wednesday, February 24th, 1864
> Was on Police to Day. Policed around the Hospital and General's Quarters. Received a letter from Mary E. Elwood. Answered Fathers and Mary's.

Thursday, February 25th, 1864
> Drilled today for the first time this week. Received a letter from Rosie and answered N's. Also wrote one to Kate Dedin.

Friday, February 26th, 1864
> Was no Drill to Day – except for Recruits. The wind commenced to blow and was very blustery on Dress Parade.

Saturday, February 27th, 1864
    Received a letter from home and from M. Velotte. Also Five Dollars from Father sent in a letter.

Sunday, February 28th, 1864
    Went on Guard this morning after inspection. Had Post No. 5 in front of the Office of the Guard Quarters. Three men were put in the Guard House during my duty.

Monday, February 29th, 1864
    Did not get off Guard today until ½ past 3 PM on account of it being general muster. Day Guards were mustered at the Guard House.

March 1864

Tuesday, March 1st, 1864
> Received a letter from Brother Townsend in New Orleans. Our Company has taken their turn at Mortar Practice firing at a Target up the beach.

Wednesday, March 2nd, 1864
> Received another letter from M. E. Ellwood and wrote one to Charles Milles, Radnor, PA. Had no Drill except for Recruits.

Thursday, March 3rd, 1864
> Our Company was firing at a target in the Marshes on the North East side of the Ramparts.

Friday, March 4th, 1864
> Firing again with the Mortars this afternoon. Had Dress Parade twice only this week.

Saturday, March 5th, 1864
> Went on Guard this morning. Was picked out for No. 18 Post at the Postern for Officers. Raining at times all afternoon. Received a letter from Kate Dedin.

Sunday, March 6th, 1864
> Companies F, M, G, & H were ordered (a)way and left Last Night about 8 o'clock destination unknown. (I) Went out and down to the Baltimore wharf.

Monday, March 7th, 1864
> Sixteen men detailed from this Company for Guard in Consequence of those four Companies leaving. Wrote Kate Dedin an answer to her letter of March 5th, 1864.

Tuesday, March 8th, 1864
> The Companies that left all returned except Company G this afternoon. Raining all Day. Was no Drill or Parade. Two Hundred recruits arrived and were the centerpiece of our Entertainment.

Wednesday, March 9th, 1864
> Was awakened in the night by A. Robertson for to take his place on Guard as he was sick. Only had four hours to stand.

Thursday, March 10th, 1864
> Raining all day. Had no Policing today as was Supernumerary and had to take the Place of a sick Guard. Received a letter from Rosie and answered N.

Friday, March 11th, 1864
> Received a letter from Kate Dedin. Raining all Day, prevented any Drill. Did not Drill any this week.

Saturday, March 12th, 1864
> Received a letter from Home. Ed. & Joe were on Guard and I was left by myself to scrub out the tent and clean up. Wrote a letter to Ed. Normall.

Sunday, March 13th, 1864
> The Weather nice and warm. Laid around Camp all Day. Was detailed with J. Noll out to go to Norfolk with Blockade running in the evening. Returned at 1 o'clock AM.

Monday, March 14th, 1864
> Still warm and clear. Drilled with Company on the Ramparts at the Iron Carriaged guns. Received a letter from F. M. Brooke.

Tuesday, March 15th, 1864
> Wrote a letter to F. M. Brooke in relation to the Bounty from Delaware County[10].

Wednesday, March 16th, 1864
> The usual Day for Battalion Drill but drilled only by Company in the afternoon on the Ramparts at the heavy Guns.

Thursday, March 17th, 1864
> Drilled this forenoon on the Ramparts at Iron Carriage Guns, was none in the afternoon. Had Dress Parade for orders. Cold!

Friday, March 18th, 1864
> Corp. Gamble & Privates Williams, Willard, Williamson, Hale, Abel, Allen & myself were detailed as a guard to go to Baltimore after Rebel Prisoners. Started at 8 o'clock from the Warf at the Fort.

Saturday, March 19th, 1864
> Arrived at Baltimore at noon after a very disagreeable Passage of 17 hours. Proceeded up the Patapsco River to (get) coal. After loading coal and some water started for the Boston Warf and loaded the Prisoners. Were 106 in Number.

Sunday, March 20th, 1864
> Started back this morning at 8 o'clock. Arrived at Point Lookout[11] where we landed our Prisoners and started back for the Fort. Having no fun. We passed a most miserable time as it was cold.

Monday, March 21st, 1864
> Arrived in Hampton Rhoads at 1 o'clock this night and anchored in the morning at 9 o'clock. We were taken off to the Warf in a Tug.

Tuesday, March 22nd, 1864
> Commenced snowing and continued all night blowing as the likes, perfect Hurricane.

Wednesday, March 23rd, 1864
> Went on Guard this morning. About 6 inches snow on the ground. Very disagreeable and cold standing Guard.

Thursday, March 24th, 1864
> Came off guard. Sun came out and snow melted making a ground of slush and water. No Drill or Parade.

Friday, March 25th, 1864
> Edward McCluen and myself went and joined the new infantry Regiment raising[12]. Went under McNeil[13] at their Promise of 1st and 2nd Corporal. J.E. Palmer went also so now our tent is empty.

Saturday, March 26th, 1864
>Men assembled on the Battery around 2 o'clock. All the men joining the new Regiment and marched out to camp at Hamilton[14] and encamped linking with my old Company. Rained all night.

Sunday, March 27th, 1864
>Was engaged with John (Palmer) in making out the Roll of the company in Lt. McNeil's Tent.

Monday, March 28th, 1864
>We engaged in sorting our tents in our Company until 10 o'clock. Sent to the Major as clerk until he obtained one.

Tuesday, March 29th, 1864
>At the Major's Headquarters making out Roll of the Regiment. Numerous other things appertaining to the formation of the same. Was relieved this evening and ordered to report to the Company in the morning.

Wednesday, March 30th, 1864
>Reported as ordered to the Ordinence Sergeant & put on Duty with a Squad of 6 men going around the tents and cleaning up.

Thursday, March 31st, 1864
>Was detailed to Policing the camp and in charge of arranging the Tents. Yesterday when I arrived Lt. Reen excused Austin and myself from drilling.

April 1864

Friday, April 1st, 1864
> Went to work. Sent some of us back & ordered us Policing. After clear this morning commenced rain this afternoon. Drilling with arms this evening.

Saturday, April 2nd, 1864
> Commenced raining this morning and continued all Day without interruption and rained in the night. Misty.

Sunday, April 3rd, 1864
> Peter Gamble and H.T. Farnsworth came out to camp and we went with them over to Hampton Bridge and returned by the Soldiers Burying Ground[15].

Monday, April 4th, 1864
> No Drill this forenoon. This afternoon Jos. Potter, Edward McCluen & myself visited the Soldiers Burying Ground and seen the Darkie troops[16] drilling.

Tuesday, April 5th, 1864
> Received two letters. One from Kate Dedin with photograph enclosed & the other from F.M. Brooke in relation to the Delaware County Bounty which he is to get for me & others.

Wednesday, April 6th, 1864
> Wrote a letter home but have not sent it having no envelopes. Went on Guard for the first time since we came to this camp. Still continues cloudy and threatening rain.

Thursday, April 7th, 1864
> Came off Guard this morning and went down to the Fort. Went in Peter Gamble's Tent and wrote 2 letters. One to Rosie and the other to F.M. Brooke. Our Lt. McNeil was ordered to Co. H. of this Regiment. Cleared off a bit.

Friday, April 8th, 1864
> On Police today digging Trenches around the Camp. Received two letters, one from Rosie & the other from home – answered Rosie's and wrote one to Kate Dedin.

Saturday, April 9th, 1864
> McCluen is on Guard this morning. Clouded up and commenced to rain and continued on at intervals all Day and night. Received Del.(aware) Co.(unty) Paper.

Sunday, April 10th, 1864
> Made Company Clerk and entered upon my duties at once. My first duty was to make our report of a Brand of survey of which the Captain of this Company is Received.

Monday, April 11th, 1864
> Still engaged in making out those reports and numerous other things. Am excused from Drill but not from Roll Call. Captain is officer of the Day.

Tuesday, April 12th, 1864
> Finished making out the report and ending them ready to send into Headquarters – Captain went into the Fort and stayed all afternoon.

Wednesday, April 13th, 1864
> Received our pay this morning and forty dollars of the Governments Bounty. Had to make out 3 more reports for there was a mistake in the others. Finished them this afternoon.

Thursday, April 14th, 1864
> Received a letter from F.M. Brooke stating that He had prepared our bounties and wrote him a letter of thanks. Also wrote a letter Home and also to G. Milles.

Friday, April 15th, 1864
> Had to make out three more reports as there was a error in the rest. Went to the Fort and Expressed my Chest home and sent forty Dollars in a letter home.

Saturday, April 16th 1864
> Raining heavy all Day at times. Received a letter from home and one from E. Howell. Answered E. Howell's. Engaged in making out forms for requisitions.

Sunday, April 17th, 1864
> Made out a Furlough for Louis Williamson this morning as he received a telegraphic stating his Wife is lying at the point of Death. Raining at times all afternoon.

Monday, April 18th, 1864
> Williamson failed to get his Furlough as the Adjunct General refused to sign it. Issued arms to the men today. All complete.

Tuesday, April 19th, 1864
> Received two letters, one from home and one from Rosie. Answered her letter. Got my Photograph taken. Gave a dollar for it. Did not do much to Day.

Wednesday, April 20th, 1864
> Wrote a letter home and sent my Photograph in it. Williamson obtained his furlough by some intervention of the Captain and started home this evening.

Thursday, April 21st, 1864
> Doing little or nothing or nothing today. Wrote a letter to my Friend Isaac Johnson this forenoon. A Brigade of Colored Troops arrived from Yorktown this afternoon followed by 3 Regiments. Arrived some time during the night.

Friday, April 22nd, 1864
> Drew clothing and distributed to the Company and was engaged in that employment nearly all Day.

Saturday, April 23rd, 1864
> Company Drill this afternoon. Went down to the Fort to get the description list of the Company but failed as there was to Many getting (them).

Sunday, April 24th, 1864
> Received a letter from Kate S. Dedin. Was over with Ed. McCluen & J. Jeffers to see the Colored Brigade inspected. Rained in the evening.

Monday, April 25th, 1864
> Lt. Reen and myself went to the Fort and was occupied in getting description Roll all Day. Was very warm. Our Regiment received by Gen. Butler's staff.

Tuesday, April 26th, 1864
> Went myself to the Fort after descriptive Roll, returned in the afternoon. Was occupied until 11 o'clock in the evening. Wrote a letter to Mary Velotte. Received marching orders.

Wednesday, April 27th, 1864
> Engaged today in making out the descriptive and muster Rolls of the Company. Getting ready for march in the morning. Corporal Joseph Pitt deserted.

Thursday, April 28th, 1864
> Marched this morning on our March to Yorktown about 8 o'clock. Pushed on within 11 miles of the place were we encamped in a large field all night.

Friday, April 29th, 1864
> Arrived at Yorktown this forenoon and encamped in a large Peach Orchard below the 9th Wisconsin, 139th New York and some Batteries of Artillery[17].

Saturday, April 30th, 1864
> Was engaged in making out pay & description Roll. Accompanied by Lt. Reinboth and Capt. Dickson[18], drew Indian Rubber Blankets & Shelter Tents. Rained all afternoon.

May 1864

Sunday, May 1st, 1864
: Received marching orders with orders to turn in our Knapsacks and everything but our shelter tents & Rubber Blankets & Gun. Also 40 Rounds of Ammunition. To move tomorrow.

Monday, May 2nd, 1864
: Knapsack did not go away today. Rained in the night and stormed very hard. Had no Blanket and passed a very miserable night.

Tuesday, May 3rd, 1864
: Still engaged in making out the Pay Rolls. Knapsack went this afternoon. It is said to arrive Norfolk. 4 days Rations issued to the men. Engaged in getting ready for going away in the morning.

Wednesday, May 4th, 1864
: Embarked on Board transport at Yorktown for someplace unknown. Suppose there was a division of us run down to Fortress Monroe and anchored in Hampton Roads at sundown.

Thursday, May 5th, 1864
: Started up the James River this morning. A man fell overboard and drowned in the night. Belonged to Co(mpany) A.[19] Ran into a Steamer and ran aground about 10 miles up. Pulled off in the evening.

Friday, May 6th, 1864
: Started this morning after getting another Pilot up the River. Overtook a main of vessels in tow of a Steamer and we also hooked on to him. Landed 1 mile above City Point at a place called "Hundred"[20]. Marched to our camp into a dense Forrest. A distance of 5 miles from the landing. Very hot and dusty.

Saturday, May 7th, 1864
: Still in the woods with orders to move at a moments notice. Part of our division made a attack on the Rebel Command fortifications at Petersburg. Succeeding in getting possession after being repelled once. Loaded our pieces at Roll call.

Sunday, May 8th, 1864
: Remained in Camp all Day. No movement of any kind among the troops in our division. Received marching orders to move in the morning at 4 o'clock AM.

Monday, May 9th, 1864 and Tuesday, May 10th, 1864
: Was up at 3 o'clock getting ready to move and one Day's Rations. Our whole Brigade marched out at 5 o'clock in Company with 12 Pieces of Artillery. Went 3 miles and then drawn up in line of Battle. No opposition. Pushed our way to Petersburg. Laid a heavy firing all Day. Reached the Railroad and commenced to tear up the rails & burn the Ties. Tore up some 2 miles of it when we had to retreat suddenly. Reached our camp in the evening. Very tired.

Wednesday, May 11th, 1864
: Rested all Day until 2 PM when we were moved into a new Camp in an open field. Thunderstorms came up in the evening. Was awakened about 12 to get ready to move in the morning.

Thursday, May 12th, 1864
> Was awakened again this morning about ½ 1 o'clock for the Company to go down and load wounded on board the Steamer "News of Jersey"[21]. Left in the morning at daylight and proceeded down the river. At a landing unloaded a Cargo of Guts.

Friday, May 13th, 1864
> The Brigade moved to the front this morning. Our Company is detailed to unload the Barge at the landing and moved our Camp to that place. Received News of our Regiment being engaged with the Rebels at Petersburg. Had 12 killed & 24 wounded.

Saturday, May 14th, 1864
> Unloaded 2600 bags of oats and cut down trees for a boundary road at the landing. Our Brigade has forced back the Rebels to Fort Darling[22] which place they are besieging. Raining at times all Day.

Sunday, May 15th, 1864
> Received a letter from Rosie. Still raining at times and every thing is muddy. Nothing done today and nothing happened of interest except news from our Regiment which is good.

Monday, May 16th, 1864
> Our Regiment along with the Brigade was surprised & attacked By Rebels in the Neighborhood of Fort Darling and compelled to fall back losing over 60 killed and wounded. Capt. Shinkle[23] mortally wounded.

Tuesday, May 17th, 1864
> The Brigade came in this evening. Was up at the Hospital looking after our wounded. Am very bad with the Diarrhea and can not eat anything. Raining almost every few hours. Wrote a letter home. Feel very bad and weak.

Wednesday, May 18th, 1864
> Went up to the doctors this morning and He gave me 3 opium[24] Pills with a drink of Brandy. Do not feel much better, running in the night every once (in) awhile. The Rebels attempted to out flank us along the river but were repulsed by Gun boats.

Thursday, May 19th, 1864
> Went again this morning to the doctors. Feel a little better. Excused from Duty.

Friday, May 20th, 1864
> Did not go to the doctors and went on Duty today. Unloading a Schooner of Hay. Very hot. The Rebels made an attack on our lines in the night but were repulsed.

Saturday, May 21st, 1864
> The Rebels made an assault on our lines near the center but were repulsed. The Cannonading & Musketry were very heavy for some 30 minutes. Went on Guard this morning. Found the body of Wm. Carel.[25]

Sunday, May 22nd, 1864
> Came off Guard this morning. Received a letter from Home. Still keep very hot. Recovered the Body of Wm. Carel who was drowned and buried him last evening.

Monday, May 23rd, 1864
> Sergeant Jeffers obtained a pass and went down to City Point to see his brother. Returned in the evening. Unloaded the balance of Oats on Board the Schooner.

Tuesday, May 24th, 1864
> Hot as ever. Went with 4 men up to the Regiment at Quarter Masters and drew Shoes & Blouses for the Company. Working at the Barge unloading Oats. Wrote a letter Home & one to Kate S. Dedin.

Wednesday, May 25th, 1864
> Finished unloading the Barge of Oats this afternoon. Unloaded some Quarter Master Stores off the <u>Metamora</u>.[26] Thunderstorm came up while loading horses on the Steamer and poured down rain.

Thursday, May 26th, 1864
> Received two letters, one from Kate S. Dedin and the other from Edwin Normall. Went on Guard this morning. Capt. Dickson went down to Burnsides Headquarters. Moved the Captain's Tent.

Friday, May 27th, 1864
> Came off Guard and went by the entrenchments. Our Captain (was) moved someplace else. It appears, to be a General. Moving forwards evacuating our works and moving to some other point.

Saturday, May 28th, 1864
> Was employed all Day unloading a Schooner & had to work all night. The men are nearly tired out working all Day & night. Rained about 10 o'clock. Getting ready to evacuate this place. Feel very tired.

Sunday, May 29th, 1864
> Went to work again this morning and finished by 10 o'clock AM. Orders came for us to get ready to move tomorrow. Slept very near all Day as I was very tired.

Monday, May 30th, 1864
> We loaded Quarter Master Steamer this forenoon. After dinner received orders to make ready to move in the evening. Had to move 2000 Boxes of hard tack. Did not get to pack our Company. Started this evening.

Tuesday, May 31st, 1864
> Left this morning on boats from the landing. Reached the James River about 9 A.M. where we were taken in tow by a large steamer and started down the river.

June 1864

Wednesday, June 1st, 1864
> Started this morning from our anchorage and moved down the River. Reached Hampton Roads at 1 PM. Came to (about) & Capt. Dickson, Lt. McNiel & myself went for pay but the Steamer sailed and left us behind.

Thursday, June 2nd, 1864
> It was Monday morning we started & not Tuesday. I made a mistake. We arrived here night before last on the Mail Boat "J. Tucker"[27]. Encamped here. Buckley[28] came in this evening. Seen J. Taylor.

Friday, June 3rd, 1864
> Encamped along the landing. Fighting is hard going on in front. We have little or nothing to do or get. Wrote two letters, one Home & the other to Rosie. Went on Guard this evening.

Saturday, June 4th, 1864
> News from our Regiment today. Several of the wounded being evacuated came in and reports it having lost 20 or 30 men. Broke camp this afternoon and went about a mile down the River & set up Camp.

Sunday, June 5th, 1864
> Raining at times. Unloaded the Balance of Oats remaining on Board the Schooner. McNiel went up to the 9th Corps Hospital this afternoon to see our wounded. (He) seen, Lt. Cassidy & Breel and several more.

Monday, June 6th, 1864
> Was up to the Hospital and seen Joe Taylor who is Brigade surgeon in charge of the 9th Corps. Hospital. The wounded still coming in from our Regiment. Went on Guard this morning. Raining in the evening.

Tuesday, June 7th, 1864
> Came off Guard this morning from Picketts. Went up to the Hospital and seen several of our wounded loaded on board Steamers. McCluen made Sergeant.

Wednesday, June 8th, 1864
> Received a package of letter paper from Home. Also a letter from Rosie last evening. Wrote a letter to Ed. Normall and to Joe Velotte. The heavy Cannonading on our left still continues, more steady.

Thursday, June 9th, 1864
> Wrote a letter to Mary Velotte & to Wm. White. Received a letter from Brother Townsend date(d) May 1st at Alexandria, La. Went on Camp Guard this morning.

Friday, June 10th, 1864
> Came off Guard this morning. Williamson went to the Hospital and I took his place as acting Quarter Master Sergeant and moved my Quarters to the Cook House.

Saturday, June 11th, 1864
> Engaged in fixing up the Cook House and arranging things in some kind of order. Clouds headed up in the Afternoon and rained very hard. Received orders to get ready to move in the morning at 4 o'clock.

Sunday, June 12th, 1864
> Did not get off until 9 or 10 o'clock and went with our Corp. about 4 miles to the front & halted in a large yard alongside of a House Landing. 18 men of our Company were detailed to take horses to the front & Austin was placed under arrest for drunkenness.

Monday, June 13th, 1864
> Moved down to our old place this morning and received orders to get ready to embark on a transport. Did not get on until 4 P.M. Run down as far as West Point[29].

Tuesday, June 14th, 1864
> Started this morning at daylight and run around up the James River until dark & anchored. Took a boat & run over to our shore with the balance of the Sugar & Coffee to the rest of the Company.

Wednesday, June 15th, 1864
> Started again at daylight and run up as far as the mouth of the Appomattox. By 4 P.M. went up that river about 2 miles to a landing. Remained on board all night. Rations run out today.

Thursday, June 16th, 1864
> The Company landed at noon. Myself and 2 others remained on board in charge of the things before going to the Company. Went back up the river to the Post Commissary after Rations.

Friday, June 17th, 1864
> Took a Boat and went again after Rations. Got everything but Coffee as they cannot get it until this evening. Started at 4 P.M. after Coffee and our 3 day Rations. Bought a Ham at the Post Commissary.

Saturday, June 18th, 1864
> Made out a Requisition for 7 Days Rations. Moore took the Hospital wagon & crossed the pontoon bride aboard but could not get back. Had to ferry our Stuff over the river in a boat. Had to leave Singles and the Horse there all night.

Sunday, June 19th, 1864
> Sent Geiser after the Balance of the Rations. Singles and the Horse returned this morning. Wrote a letter to Rosie this forenoon. Was promoted to a Sergeant. Austin, Baxter & Joyce reduced in the ranks.

Monday, June 20th, 1864
> Austin reinstated as Sergeant. Received orders to report with the Balance of the Company to Capt. Gregg across the river and marched over after dinner and was ordered back right away. Lt. Reinboth & 12 men detailed as Guard with 4 Days Rations. Very hot & Dusty.

Tuesday, June 21st, 1864
> Our Corp. recrossed the Appomattox River again this morning for the front & marched in the direction of Petersburg. Heavy cannonading in the direction of Fort Darling.

Wednesday, June 22nd, 1864
> The cannonading began last evening and continued all night without intermission. It is said the Rebel rained on Fort Darling and we had to fall back to our lines.

Thursday, June 23rd, 1864

    This afternoon fighting commenced at Petersburg. All Day the continual sound of Artillery & Muskets was enough to awaken the Dead that was killed. Went out after cherries toward evening.

Friday, June 24th, 1864

    Started this morning in Company with Geiser and Singles to obtain Rations for 6 days. Received 2 days Rations of fresh bread. Very hot & Sultry as well as dusty.

Saturday, June 25th, 1864

    Still appears to get hotter. The air is most oppressive. The fighting at Petersburg still continues. The roar of Artillery is loud and heard from a distance of 6 miles.

Sunday, June 26th, 1864

    Still hotter then it was yesterday if that was possible. Everything quiet on the front and no cannonading. Some thing unusual for this day, sending my old letters home.

Monday, June 27th, 1864

    McCluen received a letter from his mother stating that his Brother, who was wounded near this place, had died the 6th of this month at the Chesapeake Hospital[30] & was buried from there.

Tuesday, June 28th, 1864

    Lt. Reen and his Detachment that was on duty here at the Quarter Master Department received orders to report 10th Regiment in the morning. Received a letter from Rosie with Photographs enclosed.

Wednesday, June 29th, 1864

    Lt. Reen & men left this morning for our Regiment on the front. Wrote a letter to Rosie this afternoon. A great deal cooler and looks more like rain which we need badly.

Thursday, June 30th, 1864

    Obtained a team (of horses) and went over the river & drew ten Days Rations. Accompanied by Geiser. Drew 10 days of fresh Bread & 1 (day) of Beef.

July 1864

Friday, July 1st, 1864
: The first of this month was ushered in hot & Sultry with Scarcely a Breath of air. Some of the thermometers stood at 103° Degrees in the Shade. Sergeant Major Davis came down.

Saturday, July 2nd, 1864
: Drew expenses. Hotter weather then it was yesterday. So hot had it not been for a wind it would have been insufferable.

Sunday, July 3rd, 1864
: Sunday passed very quietly, very little cannonading during the Day. It commenced in the night and continued for 3 hours, very heavy. Continues to be intensely hot.

Monday, July 4th, 1864
: The fourth passed quietly with the exception of a Salute fired by the Gunboats. No cannonading going on between our forces & the enemy. Received orders to report to the Regiment in the morning.

Tuesday, July 5th, 1864
: Sands came back. His team went over the river after the balance of Bread due but had to take <u>hard tack</u> as there was no fresh Bread. Started at 2 P.M. for the Regiment and joined it at 5 & went to the front. Work in the evening and was in charge of the camp.

Wednesday, July 6th, 1864
: Moved the cooks out near the Regiment as it was too far from here to carry the rations. Hamilton returned to duty to the Company & Theo Collison was detailed in his place.

Thursday, July 7th, 1864
: Went out to the Regiment at the Rifle Pitts. Tried to draw Rations as they were out of meat. They were to be delivered tonight but have to remain until Saturday night.

Friday, July 8th, 1864
: The heat is most intense. Went again to hunt for meat. Spengler, the Quarter Master of our Regiment drew Whiskey for the Company but no Rations. Sent Vanleer to the Company.

Saturday, July 9th, 1864
: The Brigade was relieved this evening and went into (the) rear. Camped in a Woods about 1 mile towards the front. Rebel Fort Clifton[31] opened on our Battery on the hill above us but was soon stilled.

Sunday, July 10th, 1864
: The sick and all the rest were moved to our new Camp this morning. Dr. Kern's[32] resignation was accepted and sent in today. He was the Chief Surgeon of our Regiment. Heat still intense.

Monday, July 11th, 1864
: The Brigade was reviewed today at 9 A.M. by Col. Henry & Staff. Turned over the Box of Arms to the Ordinance Office. After the Brigade left the Camp for the hills the Rebs commenced Shelling them & our camp. Did not go out with them.

Tuesday, July 12th, 1864
: Remained in Camp all Day. The heat still most intense to be in tent. Was out of the camp in the afternoon. Came back towards evening.

Wednesday, July 13th, 1864
> Geisen came back to camp with orders from the Captain to report to the Company. Went over to the Ordinance Office & then reported.

Thursday, July 14th, 1864
> A Brigade moved into the Pitts along side of us last evening & 40 of our Regiment were moved to the rear trenches but not being room for our company were moved down into the ravine were we passed the day in the hot sun.

Friday, July 15th, 1864
> Still in the ravine although 1 Sergeant, 2 Corporals & 30 men were detailed to Several Companies of the Regiment for Pickett about 10 A.M. The Rebels commenced shelling our Ravine & killed Sergeant Godfrey of the Pioneers. He was almost cut in two. Relieved this evening.

Saturday, July 16th, 1864
> Engaged the principal part of this forenoon in Washing & Cleaning up for inspection. We have inspection three times a Day when off Duty.

Sunday, July 17th, 1864
> Sunday was passed in getting ready to go to the trenches. Started for them about Dark. The Rebels through a few Shells at us. Received a letter from Phebe Sharpless & one from Ann J. Harvey

Monday, July 18th, 1864
> Our Company occupies a short line of works firing across the Rail Road & City Point Pike. Went on Duty tonight as Sergeant of the Pickett. Line withdrew at daybreak & Lt. Shorburn was killed this forenoon.

Tuesday, July 19th, 1864
> Received a letter from Wm. White. Rained nearly all Day and was very muddy & unpleasant in the Pitts. Sharpshooters keep up still a continual fire with some mortar firing.

Wednesday, July 20th, 1864
> Received two letters, one from Rosie & the other from Peter Gamble at Fort Monroe. Heavy firing from our Batteries at the Rebel Works this afternoon. Rained at times.

Thursday, July 21st, 1864
> Cleared off by noon. Sun came out. The Rebels in front of us & ourselves agreed not to shoot at each other but the surrounding Batteries are continually fighting. Detail relieved this evening.

Friday, July 22nd, 1864
> The Day in Camp passed away quietly interspersed with the occurring excitements a Camp is capable to. Moved the Cooks. Had dress Parade at 6 o'clock.

Saturday, July 23rd, 1864
> Washed my shirt & Stockings this forenoon. Drew a new Pair of Pants & Pair of Stockings. Had Dress Parade at 6 o'clock and then Packed up for to relieve the Brigade in the trenches. Our Regiment remaining in the ravine. Heavy cannonading in the night.

Sunday, July 24th, 1864
> We passed this day in the ravine. Our Captain in command of the Regiment. Clouded up in the afternoon and commenced to rain at Dark & continued nearly all night. The rain is coming in the tent & wetting us.

Monday, July 25th, 1864
> Received a letter from Mary Velotte this morning. Cleared off about 10 o'clock. Cannonading commenced toward evening. Relieved this evening.

Tuesday, July 26th, 1864
> Was no inspection until afternoon and was inspected by the Colonel. Wrote a letter home to Father & sent the Certificate of my Enlistment[33] for to get some money Due from the State Government.

Wednesday, July 27th, 1864
> Washed a pair of Stockings and a Shirt this forenoon. Had Dress Parade before marching to the Pitts. Occupied the same Position we did before in the Ravine.

Thursday, July 28th, 1864
> Very hot today. Little or no cannonading during the day. But in the evening when on Pickett the Rebs shelled our whole line. A great fire in Petersburg[34].

Friday, July 29th, 1864
> Very hot again today. Received a letter from Ed. Normal. Received two Days Rations this morning & with our Brigade marched way around to the 9th Corp on our left. It is said of making a attack.

Saturday, July 30th, 1864
> Marched all night & at Daylight was Posted in Rifle Pitts & the Ball was opened by the Blowing up of a Rebel fort[35]. For more then a hour every Piece of Artillery opened up on the Rebs and a charge was made by part of our Brigade. Brown was killed & Bryner wounded.

Sunday, July 31st, 1864
> Was marching around nearly all night after we left the Pitts. They finally halted us in a ravine on the right of the 9th Corp. Fixed up our Quarters which it looks like it was going to be a permanent Camp.

August 1864

Monday, August 1st, 1864
> Heat continues to be intense. Went over this morning to the old Camp after the rest of my Kit. Towards evening a sudden order came for us to leave. Packed up and Started. Marched about 1 mile down the ravine but was ordered to the Pitts. Received a letter from J.D. Velotte.

Tuesday, August 2nd, 1864
> The Day opened hot & Sultry. Sun pouring straight down on us in the Pitts. Was on Alert all night in the Expectation of a Attack. Nothing unusual because a Rebel officer deserted.

Wednesday, August 3rd, 1864
> Clouded up and rained for some few minutes in the afternoon but it does not seem to cool the air much. Received a letter from home with $5.00¢ and some Paper enclosed.

Thursday, August 4th, 1864
> Everything seems to crack so intense is the heat. I do not know what I shall do if it continues much longer. Were relieved this evening and marched back to the ravine just in rear of our line of works.

Friday, August 5th, 1864
> Hot as ever. Wrote two letters, one to Ann J. Harvey and the other home. The Rebels under took to blow up one of our forts but failed. Sharp firing of musketry for a while.

Saturday, August 6th, 1864
> Washed my Shirt this forenoon. Wrote a letter to Phebe Anna. Went to the trenches this evening and occupied the same position as we did before.

Sunday, August 7th, 1864
> Wrote a letter to Joshua H. Sharpless & wrote one for S.D. Evans to his mother. The heat today was almost suffocating. Received a Package of letter Paper & Postage Stamps & 2 Village Records[36] from home.

Monday, August 8th, 1864
> Yesterday and today was so hot two capsules (grenades) exploded. In my life the thermometer could not have been less then 112° Degrees. Were relieved this evening.

Tuesday, August 9th, 1864
> Sent a package of old letters home. Washed my Shirt & Pants this forenoon. In the afternoon wrote two letters, one to Rosie & the other to Peter Gamble. Our brigade detailed this evening to work on the works all night.

Wednesday, August 10th, 1864
> Wrote a letter J.D. Velotte and one to D.A. Vernon, Editor of the Delaware County American in reference to my Paper I subscribed for. Went to the trenches again this evening. Still we occupy our old positions in the line.

Thursday, August 11th, 1864
> There was some Wind today that helped to make it a little cooler but in the trenches the heat was over powering.

Friday, August 12th, 1864
    Our Batteries & the Rebs had a hot Artillery Dual this morning (with) the Reb Battery across the river and killed one & wounding eleven. Received a package of envelopes from home. Relieved.

Saturday, August 13th, 1864
    Still keeps hot. Washed my Shirt & Stockings this morning. Hearing cannonading going on across the river on our extreme right. Wrote a letter to M. Velotte. Went again this evening and worked all night on the forts.

Sunday, August 14th, 1864
    I never know now when Sunday comes. Passed the Day quietly considering the hot weather. We expected to move across the river but the order was countermanded & we came out to the trenches. Wrote a letter to Wm. White.

Monday, August 15th, 1864
    Occupied Pitts across the Pike & Rail Road. The heat was nearly suffocating until the rain came on. It poured down in torrents & overflowed our Camp & drowning 3 men.

Tuesday, August 16th, 1864
    Received a letter from (my) Brother Townsend at Morganzia, Louisiana. Did not clear off until afternoon. George Spout of our Company died at the Regimental Hospital today. J. Potter returned.

Wednesday, August 17th, 1864
    Commenced Raining and rained nearly all day. Did not get relieved as we expected and will have to remain for Day and perhaps longer as there is some fresh confrontations.

Thursday, August 18th, 1864
    Still continues Wet and muddy. Received a letter from Father. The Rebels opened a heavy fire from their Battery this morning at 2 o'clock A.M. Was Sergeant of the Company today.

Friday, August 19th, 1864
    Still raining at times all day. No sign of our being relieved as yet. The Rebels again opened fire from their Batteries this morning at 2 ½ o'clock A.M. The firing was very heavy.

Saturday, August 20th, 1864
    Cannonading from the Rebels Batteries over the River continuing at intervals all day. Had orders to move off to the left tonight but the order was countermanded at 10 o'clock. Drizzling rain all evening.

Sunday, August 21st, 1864
    The Rebels again opened fire. A gun in front of us opened on us with grape & cannon & spherical case shot. No injury. We opened with Musketry. Wrote to Father & Townsend.

Monday, August 22nd, 1864
    Moved last Evening off to the left and now occupy the Skirmish line in the advance works. Raining almost continually filling the trenches with water consequently several men were shot by the Reb sharp shooters.

Tuesday, August 23rd, 1864
    Cleared off this forenoon and sun came out hot. Received a letter from Rosie. Preparations were make to resist an attack that was expected from the Rebs today and night.

Wednesday, August 24th, 1864
> The Rebels did not make their intended attack and the night passed quietly. Clouded up and raining at intervals nearly all the time.

Thursday, August 25th, 1864
> Received a letter from Joshua G. Sharpless this morning. We were again shelled this afternoon to resisted a supposed attack from the Rebels. Heavy cannon fire and Mortar fire all day and all night.

Friday, August 26th, 1864
> Very hot again today. We were relieved this evening from the Line. Holding here we have been for 12 days & nights. Marched back to the Brigade. From there we reported to the 10th Corp. Marched all night through. Nearly floundered. Oft very awful, pouring rain at times.

Saturday, August 27th, 1864
> Arrived this morning about 4 o'clock. Laid down and slept until sunrise after putting up our tents. Were order to strike tents and move to further to the rear. Am not feeling well.

Sunday, August 28th, 1864
> Remained here all Day expecting to move every minute. About Dark the order came and moved into our new Camp. Feeling sick & unwell.

Monday, August 29th, 1864
> Fixed up our tent today. Still keep unwell, cannot eat anything. The regiment went on Pickett for the first time since crossing (the river).

Tuesday, August 30th, 1864
> Still fell unwell, worse if anything. Something like the fever. Wrote a letter to Rosie this forenoon. The Regiment came off Pickett.

Wednesday, August 31st, 1864
> Was going to the Hospital this morning. Captain though I should stay (in the rear) and get treatment first. Getting weaker and weaker.

September 1864

Thursday, September 1st, 1864
> They obtained an Ambulance and I went to the 18th Corp. Hospital at Point of Rocks[37]. Fell(t) very bad.

Friday, September 2nd, 1864
> Lay on the ground with nothing but a Bed tick & a Blanket. Took some medicine. Wrote a letter to Father.

Saturday, September 3rd, 1864
> Still lying here on the ground, taking some kind of disagreeable medicine. Do not feel any better of it.

Sunday, September 4th, 1864
> Was moved to more comfortable Quarters. Good Beds with Iron Bed Stead's in the 3rd Section of the 3rd Ward.

Monday, September 5th, 1864
> *(Nothing written, too sick to write.)*

The following is written along the margin of the next page: Sick in Hospital and not able to write at the time. Dated July 30th, 1865, Lynchburg, Va.

At the time I was sick in the Hospital our forces were besieging Petersburg & Richmond and to successfully reach the place where I am now (Lynchburg). I am now writing what would have them required a force of 500'000 men and who would have had to fight their way foot by foot. Just one year ago today the fort in front of Petersburg was blown up. *(Battle of the Crater)* Look where we are today & what we have accomplished under the leadership of the <u>only man</u> who could have done it, the indomitable Grant, who along with Sheridan and Sherman, we Union Soldiers believe (are) the Greatest Warriors that ever lived.

Tuesday, September 6th, 1864
> *(Nothing written, too sick to write.)*

Wednesday, September 7th, 1864
> *(Nothing written, too sick to write.)*

Thursday, September 8th, 1864
> *(Nothing written, too sick to write.)*

Friday, September 9th, 1864
> Have not been able to keep this wrote out. I lay in the hospital all the time from 3rd Sept. to the present time.

Saturday, September 10th, 1864
> I generally get up in the mornings and wash, eat my breakfast and then lie down. Doctor ordered all the Wiskey Punch[38] I could drink.

Sunday, September 11th, 1864
> Feel a little Stronger. Still give me Wiskey Punch and Quinine. Was Inspection today of the Ward by a whole batch of Doctors.

Monday, September 12th, 1864
> Still getting Stronger. Dressed myself and walked up a far as the Post office to See weather there was a letter or not. None. Blew up cold and was very cold all night. Wrote a letter.

Tuesday, September 13th, 1864
> Smith came to see me today. Pete Gamble also was to see me. Walk about a little but am very weak. Wrote a letter to B. Longaker and E.L. McCluen.

Wednesday, September 14th, 1864
> Pete came to see me again today. Gave me two Sheets Paper and two Envelopes. Received a letter from home with $5.00¢ enclosed.

Thursday, September 15th, 1864
> Sergeant Austin came to see me before he went to the Company. Wrote a letter to J.H. Sharpless. Walked over to the Sutters in the evening and purchased ½ lb. Raisins & a Apple.

Friday, September 16th, 1864
> Warm Day, flies very bad. Did not walk about much until afternoon. Walked over to the Sutters & bought ½ Pound Butter & 25 cents worth Apples. Getting Stronger but still am very weak.

Saturday, September 17th, 1864
> Went up with the rest of the patients to the Cook House for the first time today at dinner. Ed. McCluen came to see me and brought me 3 letters and a Paper. 1 letter from Rosie, 1 from M. Velotte, 1 from A(nn). J. Harvey.

Sunday, September 18th, 1864
> Answered the letters received yesterday. Bought five Sheets of Paper and five Envelopes. Also a jar of jelly for fifty-cents. Still feel a little better and getting stronger.

Monday, September 19th, 1864
> Five men were sent to the convalescent camp this morning. Wrote a letter to P.T. Hysleman for the first time since I left home. Bought another ½ lb. Butter this evening for 40¢.

Tuesday, September 20th, 1864
> Received a letter from Wm. White and answered it. J.A.M. McLaughlin[39], a Patient in this section, died this evening about Midnight with the Diarrhea.

Wednesday, September 21st, 1864
> Wrote a letter home and received a Package of Papers from Mother. John O'Brien was down from the company bringing a knapsack belonging to John McLaughlin what was his.

Thursday, September 22nd, 1864
> Received news that our Regiment is going to be paid off tomorrow. Wrote a note to E.L. McCluen and also a letter to Phebe A. Sharpless. Dresses me out in a Hospital uniform. Sent 8 men North (home) this evening.

Friday, September 23rd, 1864
> Wrote a letter to E.L. McCluen and sent it up by way one of our Nurses who went up to get paid but there was nothing of it. Joe Potter & A. Dickerson came to the Hospital this morning.

Saturday, September 24th, 1864
>Rained at several different times but finally cleared off. Find myself very near well except sever pain in the Bowels. Received a package of letter paper from home, brought down by E. Welsh. A Salute of 100 guns was fired along the line. Sheridan's victory. (*celebrating Battle of Fisher's Hill*)

Sunday, September 25th, 1864
>Very cool this morning. Went to Church about 10:00 o'clock. Wrote a letter to Ed. Normal in the evening. The Doctor came around and took my name among others to be sent back tomorrow.

Monday, September 26th, 1864
>Was loaded in Ambulance and brought down to Broadway landing where we were loaded on board the "Geo. Leary"[40] and run down to Fort Monroe & unloaded at the W. Mellan Hospital[41]. Had some 100 Yards to walk.

Tuesday, September 27th, 1864
>Doctor did not prescribe for me evidently thinking that I was well enough. Seen Hoffner who was wounded the 28th of August, (he is) very near well. Wrote a letter to E.L. McCluen.

Wednesday, September 28th, 1864
>Wrote a letter to Harry Worth in the Fort. The monotony of Hospital life is very wearisome to me now. I do not get as much as I can to eat for my appetite increases very fast. Very nice weather. Received a pair of Drawers from (the) Ward Master.

Thursday, September 29th, 1864
>Wrote a letter home again asking for money & Postage Stamps. I am entirely out. Doctor prescribed for me this morning for the first time since I came. Wiskey and something.

Friday, September 30th, 1864
>I was surprised this forenoon by a large load of wounded that was brought in from our Brigade that was engaged at Deep Bottom[42]. J. O'Brien & Donty of our Company was among the number. Hospital Steam(ship) Matilda[43] burst her Boiler at the Warf.

October 1864

Saturday, October 1st, 1864
> This morning the Doctor took down the names of all those that was not fit for Duty to send them North. Costello and Rood of my Tent is going. Doctor thinks I will be fit for Duty in a few days.

Sunday, October 2nd, 1864
> Seen J. Ryan who informed me that Corp. Beers was here & wounded. Went to see him. (He) was struck in the leg below the knee. Sergeant Myers and myself went to Chesapeake Hospital and seen Lt.'s McNiel & Reen who are wounded.

Monday, October 3rd, 1864
> Wounded are constantly arriving from the Front. A lot of Rebel wounded were brought in this afternoon. Still keeps raining & drizzling at times. 4 of us in our tent were called out to the Cook House to String Beans. Finished at – 11:00 P.M.

Tuesday, October 4th, 1864
> Walked down to the News office to get a Paper but they had sold out. Seeing more wounded belonging to our Regiment, out of Company G & A. Good News from the Front, Grant in sight of Richmond.

Wednesday, October 5th, 1864
> The Doctor came around this morning & took the names of all the rest in the Tent except myself to send them North. Lt. Reen came up to see me. (He) informed me that my Capt. H.B. Dickson was killed in the late fight. Sent a letter home.

Thursday, October 6th, 1864
> Rood, Costello, Terest & Garrit were sent North out of my Tent. I am alone now. Just a few wounded after they left. A letter came for Road. I redirected it & sent it to ------, his wife. Wrote a letter for W. Hoffner. Sergeant Myers gave me 55 cents. Costello game me 10 cents before he left.

Friday, October 7th, 1864
> Sergeant Myers & myself went down to see Sergeant McElrath of Company B of our Regiment who was wounded in the late battles. Went down to the Store in the evening after Soap along with Wm. Hoffner.

Saturday, October 8th, 1864
> Feel very lonesome now since the other left. Lt. Reen came in for to see me this afternoon. Received a letter from Father with $10.00¢ enclosed.

Sunday, October 9th, 1864
> Nothing occurred to break the monotony of Hospital life. Blew up cold towards night and continued (to) blow during the whole night.

Monday, October 10th, 1864
> The first cold spell this fall was this morning. Went down to the Fort but could not get inside. Came back and wrote a letter home acknowledging the receipt of the $10.00¢.

Tuesday, October 11th, 1864
> Quite warm again. Wrote a letter for John O'Brien, also one for myself to Rosie. Hicks received a letter in the evening from C.S. Rood – he is in at York Harbor[44].

Wednesday, October 12th, 1864
> Wrote an answer to Road's letter. Went to nursing this afternoon for one of the Nurses who is sick. Sergeant Myers and myself went down town in the Evening to see the sights.

Thursday, October 13th, 1864
> Was called up at 12:00 by Miller watched until 6 this morning. Fell very unwell all Day being in bed all afternoon. Received a letter from home.

Friday, October 14th, 1864
> Today is my 22nd birthday and since my last birthday I have seen more that I value then all the rest of life put together. Wrote a letter to the 1st Sergeant of my Company[45].

Saturday, October 15th, 1864
> Wrote a letter for Benliss. He is a nurse in this section. In the evening us Patients was moved to the wooden wards.

Sunday, October 16th, 1864
> Passed a restless night, having a severe pain in the stomach. In the afternoon went in Ward 13 to see Christy of our company who had his arm taking off in the fight at Chaffin's Farms.

Monday, October 17th, 1864
> The weather is yet nice and warm having had no cold blow up but twice this fall that lasted but one Day. A man died in this ward in the evening.

Tuesday, October 18th, 1864
> Cloudy and looked like rain nearly all Day. Went down to the Chesapeake Hospital and seen Lt. Reen who told me that (the) Paymaster was coming out to pay us off. C.H. Moore left.

Wednesday, October 19th, 1864
> Paymaster came up and Paid me six months Pay $138.00¢ & one installment of Bounty. Received a letter from E.L. McCluen in the Evening. A man died this morning. Made application for a furlough.

Thursday, October 20th, 1864
> Wrote home to Father and sent $30.00¢ in the letter. Also answered E.L. McCluen letter of yesterday. Wrote a letter to Peter Gamble.

Friday, October 21st, 1864
> It is now the third day since I made application for a Furlough but have heard nothing from it yet. I am getting tired of this place. It is lonesome.

Saturday, October 22nd, 1864
> Bought a Watch from Wesley Washburn[46] on the 20th. Which I forgot to make note of on that Day. Paid him $9.00¢ for it. Blustery and getting colder.

Sunday, October 23rd, 1864
> Quite cold last night and this morning. Wind blowing from the North West. Wrote a letter to Cousin Phebe Anna. Went Down to C(amp) Hamilton.

Monday, October 24th, 1864
> Little cool this morning but moderated during the day and was warm.

Tuesday, October 25th, 1864
> Received a letter from Ed McCluen from the front. Was very unwell all Evening. Vomiting and a severe pain in the Bowels.

Wednesday, October 26th, 1864
> Petterson who had his bed next to mine and was sent to his Regiment this morning took my Pipe & Tobacco. Wrote to Ed. (McCluen). Feel very unwell all Day.

Thursday, October 27th, 1864
> Wrote a letter to Rosie also received a letter from Wm. White. Peter Gamble came down to this Hospital today. Loaned him $5.00¢. Bought a pair of Pants, price $5.50¢.

Friday, October 28th, 1864
> Peter and myself went down Town this morning and got our Breakfast. Came back and Wrote a letter to Wm. White.

Saturday, October 29th, 1864
> Peter and myself went down again at Dinner and had Apple Dumplins. I have nothing to do but spend my money which I do rather greedy.

Sunday, October 30th, 1864
> Took the Car this morning & went down to Camp Hamilton. After I came back the Doctor visited us and took the names of eleven of us for a Furlough of fifthteen Days.

Monday, October 31st, 1864
> The Furloughs that was expected to arrive this afternoon did not come. A wounded man died this morning in this Ward from its effects.

November 1864

Tuesday, November 1st, 1864
> This Day passes and nothing of interest to write. The still same monotony of lonesome & tiresome Hospital life.

Wednesday, November 2nd, 1864
> Today wrote a letter to Joshua H. Sharpless who resides at Wilmington, Delaware. Passed the Day as usual, nothing to do but run around.

Thursday, November 3rd, 1864
> Received two letters this Evening, one from Ed. Normall and one with Electoral Tickets in from someone unknown. Nursing all Day. Some Furloughs arrive and some went home.

Friday, November 4th, 1864
> Received my Furlough this morning and Started for Baltimore at 3 P.M. in the Steamer "Adelaide[47]" along with Peter Gamble and nearly 1000 others Furloughed Soldiers.

Saturday, November 5th, 1864
> Arrived in Baltimore at 7 A.M. this morning and took the cars for Wilmington, Del at 9 which place arrived at 1 P.M. Came up home with Thomas Poole. Blew up very cold.

Sunday, November 6th, 1864
> Was at home all day did not feel very well all Day. Things looked as usual since I went away.

Monday, November 7th, 1864
> Raining this morning. Got ready and went up to Fairville with Ben Armstrong. Remained all night at Uncle Jacob's[48]. Rained nearly all Day.

Tuesday, November 8th, 1864
> Still raining. Left Fairville and went to Media and hired a horse to go to Radnor and voted came back to J.D. Velotte and stayed all night. Rain pouring down.

Wednesday, November 9th, 1864
> Went up to Ammon Eachus after Dinner. Ed & I went up to Leon James[49] Store. Still keeps raining. I took Joe[50] to the station who was going to Lewisburg.

Thursday, November 10th, 1864
> After Breakfast Saddled Joe's Horse and went to Media. Came around by Felix Velotte's. Cleared off this afternoon.

Friday, November 11th, 1864
> Went to Media and took the cars for Philadelphia. Met Peter Gamble in the Evening. Went to Charles Milles & stayed all night.

Saturday, November 12th, 1864
> After Breakfast, Peter & myself went to the "Farmers Market". Seen several of the Radnor Farmers. Clouded up after Dinner in the Evening. Started for Media in the cars. Met Pen Velotte and went up to J.(oe) G.'s.

Sunday, November 13th, 1864
> Ed Normall came down this forenoon. J.G. came home last Evening. Cleared off cold. Pen & I after Dinner went Down to his father's & came back about 7 o'clock.

Monday, November 14th, 1864
    Left Joe's this morning for the cars and came to Fairville to Uncle Jacob's. Remained there until 3 ½ o'clock then started home which place I arrived near Dark. Very Cold.

Tuesday, November 15th, 1864
    Clouded up and commenced to Hail and finally turned to rain which continued nearly all Day. Cleared off in the evening. Cold.

Wednesday, November 16th, 1864
    Went up to John Sharpless this forenoon and took Dinner.

Thursday, November 17th, 1864
    Cloudy and looked like rain in the afternoon. Along with Maris Dixon went up to Joe Poole's. Husking and helped haul in the Corn.

Friday, November 18th, 1864
    Cloudy & rained nearly all Day.

Saturday, November 19th, 1864
    Still raining and appears to look as much like continuing longer. Getting lonesome again.

Sunday, November 20th, 1864
    Not raining this morning but still cold & cloudy. Will Phillips & myself went over to Dixon's in the forenoon. Commenced to rain in the evening.

Monday, November 21st, 1864
    Arose this morning at 6 o'clock & Father took me to Wilmington to go back. Started at 10 A.M., arrived in Baltimore at 3 P.M., left for Fort Monroe at 5 P.M.

Tuesday, November 22nd, 1864
    Wrote a letter to Rosie. Did not meet Peter until this morning just as we arrived at Fort Monroe. Raining as fast as ever. Reported at the office & was sent to Ward 12 as before. Wrote a letter to Father.

Wednesday, November 23rd, 1864
    Received my discharge from the Hospital and in company with some 200 were sent off to our Regiment. Embarked onboard the Steamer "Susan"[51]. Did not arrive at the Hundreds until near 9 o'clock P.M.

Thursday, November 24th, 1864
    Remained in the open air all last night without Tent or fire. Very cold. Marched to my Regiment in time to get my Thanksgiving Dinner. Found the Regiment encamped on Chaffin's Farm[52].

Friday, November 25th, 1864
    Wrote a letter to Father and one to Rosie. Have not done any Duty as yet. Also wrote a letter to the Ward Master 12 & to Mary Velotte.

Saturday, November 26th, 1864
    Ed & myself was over to the 97th Regiment. Wrote a letter to Ben Long. Done nothing but carry some wood. Elwood Gilbert, Evan Thomas & Frank Stewart came down in the evening to see me. They belong to the 203rd Regiment.

Sunday, November 27th, 1864
> Very nice Day. Went over to the 203rd Regiment and seen E. Gilbert, E. Thomas F. Stewart & Several others from Delaware County I knew. Clouded up late in the afternoon and rained some.

Monday, November 28th, 1864
> Wrote a letter to S.J. Bowen, City Post Master[53], Washington D.C. Subscribed for a memorial of our Company. Henry Worth came to see us from 2nd Division Headquarters.

Tuesday, November 29th, 1864
> The weather is very mild and pleasant. Wrote a letter (to) Joseph D. Velotte. Drew 8 Pairs Shoes and issued to the Company.

Wednesday, November 30th, 1864
> Made out the original list of our Company organization for the Memorial. I am also getting made out a Duty Roster for December.

December 1864

Thursday, December 1st, 1864
>   Went down to General Pain's Headquarters[54] this forenoon to see Harry Worth & get a <.>⌐L··>·>⌐. of ⊓]⊔⊔·>]. Could not get it as he had none. He is going to bring it up tomorrow.

Friday, December 2nd, 1864
>   Harry Worth came up the forenoon and brought the ⊓]⊔⊔·>] while Ed was on drill. Harry left about Supper. Very nice weather.

Saturday, December 3rd, 1864
>   The weather continues to be mild and warm. Rumors of a move are flinging around. Received a letter from Mary Velotte.

Sunday, December 4th, 1864
>   Jesse White & Several others of the 97th Regiment came down to see Ed. We all went over to look at the captured Fort Harrison[55]. Orders came to strike tents but the order was countermanded.

Monday, December 5th, 1864
>   Orders came again this morning and we moved about 1 mile to the rear to a new camp. Very warm Day. Commenced to clear a place to build ourselves a Log house.

Tuesday, December 6th, 1864
>   The day was passed by Ed & myself in carrying logs for our new house. Wetzler got it some what near done by evening. Still keeps warm.

Wednesday, December 7th, 1864
>   Had two Days Rations cooked and issued to the men in accordance with orders issued the night before but did not move. Plastered the cracks between the Logs today. House near done.

Thursday, December 8th, 1864
>   Finished plastering our shanty and put the Roof on in the Evening. Received a letter from Father in the evening.

Friday, December 9th, 1864
>   Wrote a letter home this forenoon. The weather which has been mild for several days blew up cold this Evening and began (to) Snow and Sleet.

Saturday, December 10th, 1864
>   The ground this morning was White. The Rebels attached our Pickett's this morning & drove them. In the consequence we was called out to the scene of action but was held in reserve. Roads very muddy, remained out all night.

Sunday, December 11th, 1864
>   Passed a most disagreeable night in the Bivouac without Shelter or Blankets. Ordered back and returned to our Camp about Noon. Received a letter from Rosie and answered it this afternoon.

Monday, December 12th, 1864
>   Very cold all day.

Tuesday, December 13th, 1864
>   Wrote a letter to Edwin Normall. Still continues to be cold. The snow all gone and mud drying up.

Wednesday, December 14th, 1864
>   Building a Cook house for the company. Today very nice weather being mild and pleasant.

Thursday, December 15th, 1864
>   Finished the Cook house. Nothing unusual occurring but in the afternoon the Sound of heavy cannonading is heard in the direction of Petersburg. Wrote a letter to Phebe Anna Sharpless.

Friday, December 16th, 1864
>   Obtained a Check from the Sutler for $3.00¢. There was Regiment inspection at 2:00 P.M. I attended for the first time since rejoining the Regiment.

Saturday, December 17th, 1864
>   Very warm for this time of the Year. Wrote a letter to Mary Velotte.

Sunday, December 18th, 1864
>   There was to be inspection this morning but the rain preempted.   Raining at intervals nearly all Day. Ed went out to see some friends belonging to the 11th Pennsylvania Company.

Monday, December 19th, 1864
>   Cleared off sometime in the night. Employed in grading the Street in the afternoon. Very warm again today. Cold in the Evening.

Tuesday, December 20th, 1864
>   Received a letter from Bro. Joe with receipt of Box enclosed. Found on rising this morning and to my astonishment Meat. It had rained during the night which it continued the greater part of the Day but cleared off in the evening.

Wednesday, December 21st, 1864
>   A order was issued and read to the Company this evening in reference to the coming Christmas. Prizes are to be given to those who make the Best appearance. Our Regiment was detailed as a fatiger fa--- to build a Gundray road.

Thursday, December 22nd, 1864
>   The erection of Wreaths and Arches are under the supervision of <u>Sergeant Crahan</u> who has taken the necessary steps for their commencement. Wrote a letter to G. Miles.

Friday, December 23rd, 1864
>   Wrote a letter to Rosie this evening. Was busily engaged all Day in making our Arches & Wreaths. Very fine weather but cold.

Saturday, December 24th, 1864
>   Very cold this morning.

Sunday, December 25th, 1864
>   Inspection of Company Quarter this forenoon. The Day was passed principally in getting ready for the Farce tomorrow. Received a letter from Ed. Normall.

Monday, December 26th, 1864
> Rained in the night, consequently was very wet & muddy but not withstanding there was a Merry Christmas. The whole Regiment nearly being Drunk. The proceedings was concluded by a mock Dress Parade in which the whole Brigade participated.

Tuesday, December 27th, 1864
> Great many of the men have not go over their Christmas frolic and their appearance this morning is ludicrous in the extreme. Some lost Pants, Shoes & Caps. Still muddy & disagreeable.

Wednesday, December 28th, 1864
> Wrote a letter to Ike Johnson. Rained heavily again in the night. The roads are in a terrible condition. We were this afternoon ordered way with 2 days Rations but the order was countermanded.

Thursday, December 29th, 1864
> The Regiment was ordered out to Police around Camp but was ordered back to their Quarters for inspection of Ammunition. Blew up cold in the evening.

Friday, December 30th, 1864
> Wrote a letter to Edwin Normal. Moderate (weather) considering and looks like rain.

Saturday, December 31st. 1864
> Commenced raining in the night and continued pouring down nearly all Day. Mustered for four months pay by the Major of the 58th Regiment Payrolls.

Here the daily entries end. The following entries were made on free sheets under the paper headings.

Memoranda

Mrs. Johnson commenced washing for me the 4th of January (1864) at 21 cents per month at Fortress Monroe.

Mrs. Johnson ceased washing for me the 26th day of March, 1864. I am indebted to her for 2 months & 3 weeks of washing.

Was made 2nd Corporal of the 188 Regiment of Infantry along with Edward McCluen the 28th Day of March 1864 at Camp Hamilton.

1st (January, 1864)
(This passage was written in pencil and then ink on top. To date I have not been able to decipher more then single words.)

May 11th, 1864
    Received 3 letters, one from home, one from Ike Johnson & the other from Wm. White. Nathan Baxter sent me $5.00. Ike informed me that Ned Chase[56] received commission as Captain in a Colored Regiment.

May 14th, 1864
    Wrote to Father acknowledging the receipt of $15.00. Also to Rosie Kirk.

July 13th, 1864
    Today being in the trenches before Petersburg, the Rebels commenced Shelling us, our company being in a ravine below the City along the river. Several shells fell & Bursted amongst us, hitting Sergeant Godfrey of the Pioneer Corps cutting him nearly in two. Striking him on top of the right shoulder & smashing through coming out below the left arm. We buried him on top of the hill near a house or in the yard.

August 15th, 1864
    Rained heavily today raising the stream in the ravine in the rear of our works and completely covered every Soldier & Settler and all their Lands. I went out (left before the storm) to get Tobacco. Bought the melon for 5¢ and some Tobacco for 20¢ got everything needed for 75¢.

Captain H. B. Dickerson….*(This passage was written in pencil and then ink on top. To date I have not been able to decipher more then several names.)*

Oct. 1st & Sept. 30th, 1864

Sergeant Myers loaned me 55¢ Oct. 6th, 1864.

Loaned Theo Lush[57] $5.00¢ Oct. 19th, 1864

Loaned Peter Gamble $5.00 Oct. 27, 1864

Jan. 4th, 1865
    Received a letter from Cousin J.H. Sharpless

Jan. 5th, 1865
>Received a letter from Father.

Jan. 6th, 1865
>Received a Box from home which started the 19th of last month. Also received a P(air) of Boots and wrote a letter home.

Jan. 9th, 1865
>Received a letter from M. Velotte.

Jan. 10th, 1865
>Wrote a letter to Rosie.

Received a letter Jan 15th, 1865

Jan. 22nd, 1865
>Wrote a letter to Father

Jan. 24th, 1865
>Wrote a letter to Father and sent a Military Register. Also received a letter from him.

Marched from Danville to Patrick Court House, a distance of 75 miles, starting on the 20th and arriving at Patrick Court House 24th day of August, 1865.

September 14th, 1865
>The following named men joined my company from detached services marching from Danville to this place (Patrick Court House, Va) in a little over two days a distance of nearly 75 miles. Pack, Smith, Quinn, Harriety, Feiuoin Firestone, Fry, Bryan, Secrist, and Zimmerman.
>Received a letter from Father with $20.00¢ enclosed.

July 1st, 1866
>Borrowed $25. from Townsend (Brother)

June 10th, 1866
>Borrowed $5. from Wm. Burrell.

July 15th, 1866
>Borrowed $3. from Peter Gamble.

Aug. 1st, 1866
>Borrowed $10. from Thom. Lenoard.

Cash Account January

April 13. Received of Government 66.00

To find the circumference of circle multiply the diameter by 3.1416.

H. Williams
No. 27 Haighurst Avenue
Slead, N.J.

Cash Account February

December 14th, 1865
    Our Regiment was mustered out of service today at City Point.

December 18th, 1865
    Arrived last Saturday evening (the) 16th last from City Point and was paid off and discharged today therefore the 188th Penna. Vols ceases to exist from (this) date. Purchased a Suit of clothes which cost $100.00/100¢.

Saturday, March 3rd, 1866
    Commenced boarding at J.L. Walkers Hotel, No 2003 Market Street, Phila. at $5.00¢ per week

Cash Account March

April 23rd, 1866
    Received a letter of recommendation from J.M. Broomall[58], M. C. Chester, Delaware Counties to W.B. Thomas[59] with the object of obtaining a situation as Clerk in the Custom House at Philadelphia. Called on Mr. Thomas Wednesday morning 25th, who informed me that there was no vacancy but to call again in two weeks from date of visit.

March 1st, 1867
    Commenced work this date at Media Mills, Media, Pa for Ellwood M. Worrell[60] at $25. per month, Boarding included.

Cash Account April

House wants cementing on the outside next (to) road. Well on the outside. Old well, wants fixing up. Move shedding & 1 hen house nearer. Necessary want door though into kitchen.

(This could be the London Grove, Chester County, PA home that is listed as William H. & Roseanna Walter's home in the 1880 Census. They lived at that home until 1899 when they moved to Ward 24, Philadelphia, PA.)

Cash Account May

(This page was blank in the diary.)

Cash Account June, July, August

Lt. E.S. McCluen in account with Sergt. Wm. H. Walter

1 Blanket	7.00
2 Pr. Pants	9.50
1 " Shoes	2.70
1 Blouse	4.80
	24.00

July 26th, 1866

While on my road from my former boarding house, 5th & Chatham Street to West Phila. this Evening I stopped in a Store, Corner of 6th & Callohill to buy a Shirt and tendered in Payment a $20 note which proved to be a counterfeit. I was arrested by a police Officer and taken to the 6th District Station House and placed in a cell which would have disgraced "Libby Prison"[61]. I remained until morning when I had my hearing before Alderman Toland who after hearing the charges of the Officer and questioned whom I had passed it on and questioning me as to where I got the note hold me in $100. Bail to appear July 30th to answer the charge of Counterfeiting and then coolly asked me if I had Bail which fact he knew as well as myself. 1 ½ o'clock came and brought with it the Prison Van into that I was loaded and after riding around the City for some time finally brought up at Moyamensing[62]. I was soon shown to my room (No. 100) by the obliging Host who to keep meddlers from intruding on my privacy and probably myself intruding on somebody else's privacy kindly locked the door and barred it. In the meantime Tom Lenoard, who had learned of my incarceration, used his utmost endeavors to get me out on Bail which he accomplished on the morning of the 30th, after I had been brought back from Moyamensing to the Station House. My joy can be well imagined. I was just on the Eve of taking a Fever as I had almost worried myself sick. In the afternoon my second hearing came off when I was Honorably acquitted of the charges by my former good character. It is scarcely necessary to add that I had served five days imprisonment for a crime I was innocent of.

Cash Account September

Mr. A.S. Dial
Pemyopolis
Fayette Co, Pa

Ross R. Sterner
Addison
Somerset Co, Penna

Photographs Whitaker & Co.[63]
No. 814 Chestnut Street
Phila.
Negative Nr. 4224

Fred A Reen
Liverpool Rd
Perry Co, Pa

Cash Account October

October 25th, 1865
    Patrick Court House, Va. I am to live, (told) by B.U. Smith's prediction 32 years longer now being in my 23rd year. (Signed) Wm. H. Walter

Considering that William was 94 at the time of his death, Mr. Smith's prediction was off by 39 years!

July (no year given) sold Overcoat.

June 23rd – 26th
Union National Bank, Wilmington

Cash Account November

Account for Washing with this collection
    To this Date stub 5   1.25
    In Washington 6 Peaches @ .10   0.60
    20 Dov. 4 Dov   0.40

Peter Gamble
Manchester
Ocean Co., NJ

B.Z. Arnold
No. 1330 Lombard Street
Phila.

Cash Account December

Drew 12lbs Fresh Bread for 71 men.

June 11th, 1865
Drew 90 lbs Salt Beef and 53 lbs Pork for 72 men.

B.F. Paullin
Wood Street Above 16th
Phila.

D.W.W. Ball
Ellsworth No. 1016
Phila.

Summary of Accounts

Smith
Regen
Lutz
-----en *(The pencil is so faded it is impossible to make out this and the next name.)*
----ets
Meyer
Morre
Kelly

Jarvis Smith
Holton Co.
Maine

Memoranda

Date   **Dolls. Cts.**

Entered Richmond on the 3rd day of April, 1865. The enemy evacuated during the night.

Sunday, April 9th, 1865
    Gen. Lee surrendered his entire army of Northern Virginia to Gen. Grant today.

Pork	80 Rations	$ 60
Beef	80 "	$ 80
Sugar	80 "	$120
Coffee	80 "	$ 6 ½
Svap	80 "	$ 3 ¼
Potatoes	80"	$ 24
		$ 293.75

M. Chamerlan
No. 221 North 15th St.
Phila. PA

Amount 9 Days Rations
Pork	80 Rations	$ 60
Sugar	80 "	$120
Coffee	80 "	$ 6 ½
Svap	80 "	$ 3 ¼
Potatoes	80"	$ 24
Beef	80 "	$ 80

Amount 2 Days Rations
Pork	80 Rations	$200
Beef	80 "	$120
Sugar	80 "	$120
Coffee	80 "	$ 21
Svap	80 "	$ 6 ½
Potatoes	80"	$ 4

910 Sergeant above Race M.
(address)

K. Reade
J.P. Rashburn
Capt. Foss

204.17

C. Burnside
Kentucky
Those are the last of the entries in Williams Diary.

The 188th Pennsylvania Volunteers

William Harvey Walter enlisted: November 30, 1863; was promoted from private to corporal on December 1st, 1863; and to 2nd sergeant on June 19th, 1864; he was mustered out of service with his company on December 14, 1865.

The regiment was formed from surplus men of the 152nd Penna. or 3rd Penna. Heavy Artillery Regiment that was serving as garrison troops at Ft. Monroe, Va. and was sent to the 18th Corps of the Army of the James and was heavily engaged in the actions of the siege of Petersburg, Va. and the final Appomattox campaign. The unit remained on duty as occupation troops in Lynchburg, Va. until December of 1865.

The Third Artillery, One Hundred and Fifty-second of the line, was organized for garrison duty at Fortress Monroe. Numerous recruits were sent to it from time to time, after entering the service, and as it sustained few losses, its ranks were not only kept full, a large number of unassigned men accumulated. The number of surplus men had become so great by the first of April, 1864, that an order was issued from the War Department, directing a call to be made for volunteers from this regiment, to form a new infantry regiment. In response to the call, over six hundred men volunteered, and in less than two weeks, a new regiment, afterwards known as the One Hundred and Eighty-eighth, was organized, with nearly nine hundred men. The following field officers were appointed, promoted from captains of companies in the Third: George K. Bowen, Lieutenant Colonel, Francis H. Reichard, Major. A large proportion of the men had served in other organizations before entering the Third, over three hundred having been in the Reserve Corps The organization, arming, and equipping of the new regiment had scarcely been completed, when it was ordered to the field. On the morning of April 25th, it took up the line of march from Camp Hamilton a mile and a half from the Fortress, where the organization had been made, for Yorktown. Upon its arrival, it was assigned to the Third Brigade, First Division, of the Eighteenth Corps, where it was associated with the Second Connecticut, Fourth New Hampshire, and Fifty-eighth Pennsylvania Regiments.

On the 4th of May, the Eighteenth Corps moved by transports to Bermuda Hundred, above City Point, on the James. Skirmishing commenced soon after the debarkation, which continued for a full week before the advance reach Fort Darling, at Drury's Bluff, a strong work upon a commanding position At Proctor's Creek, on the 10th, the command was warmly engaged, losing two killed, and on the 13th and 14th, again sustained some loss. Major Reichard, who was in command of the skirmish line of the brigade ha succeeded in driving the enemy out of a small redoubt, within eight hundred yards of the fort, and had posted some of his men behind some log huts, where they picked off the enemy's gunners. During Sunday, comparative quiet prevailed, the men busying themselves in throwing up breast-works. On the morning of Monday the 16th, the enemy having massed his forces and prepared them for action, under cover of a dense fog, which hung like an impenetrable curtain on every hand, made an unexpected and most determined assault. The firing was of necessity much at random, but the struggle was maintained with unflinching valor, and positions were taken and re-taken at the point of the bayonet. The enemy bore heavily upon the right of the line, and Beckman's Brigade, which held this ground, was driven in. The Third Brigade was moved to its support, and in the midst of the movement, the right wing of the regiment, consisting of six companies, under command of Colonel Bowen, by order of Captain Reed, of General Brooks' staff; was separated from the left, and took position to the right, and considerably in advance of the rest of the brigade. Soon after taking position, Captain Reed rode forward and informed Colonel Bowen that the position was an important one, and must be held to the last extremity. Other aids came, and finally General Brooks himself, to encourage the men, and to magnify the importance of the position. Finally, Captain Reed called for volunteers to go forward a few hundred yards to bring off a Union battery that had been abandoned. The battalion responded in a body, and soon had possession of the battery, but found it so disabled, that they were unable to remove it. Discovering this movement, the enemy opened a heavy and a most murderous fire upon the command, compelling it to fall back to its first position. By this fire, Captain Hiram R. Shinkle was mortally wounded, and fell into the enemy's hands, dying while a prisoner at Richmond. As the command executed this retrograde movement, the portion of the Union line, which was posted in its rear, unfortunately mistook it for a charge of the enemy, and opened fire upon it, delivering two volleys before the mistake was discovered. The division was finally driven back and took position behind its works at Bermuda Hundred. The loss in this unfortunate engagement was eleven killed and sixty wounded. The command was immediately put to fortifying, and for a period of two weeks, it was kept busy in strengthening and improving the works.

Near the close of May, the Eighteenth Corps, under command of General Baldy Smith, was ordered to reinforce the army of the Potomac, and on the evening of the 1st of June, came up to the Sixth Corps near Cold Harbor, taking position on its right. Scarcely had the newly arrived forces got into position, when the word to advance was quietly passed along the lines, and a simultaneous and most desperate charge, by the entire Union force in position, was made on the enemy's strong lines of well abatised earth-works and forts. These proved to be well manned, and the storm of deadly missiles which was poured upon the advancing troops, caused them to recoil. Three times the lines were rallied, and returned to the attack, when, just as darkness was setting 1n, the enemy's outer line of works was carried, and though exposed until far into the night to a desperate artillery fire, was held and fortified, every spade, pick, tin cup, plate, even to the hands of the men, being brought into requisition. At a little before dawn, on the morning of the 3d, the troops were again formed, and two desperate charges were made, but all with no avail. Their ranks were swept with terrible effect, and they were compelled to desist, after having displayed unparalleled daring and courage, and left the ground strewn with their dead and wounded, many of them lying close up under the enemy's guns Falling back to their lines, they fell to fortifying and strengthening their works, and for a period of ten days, artillery was plied with little cessation, but without material effect. In the two brief struggles on the 1st and 3d, the One Hundred and Eighty-eighth lost twenty-four killed, and a large number wounded. Among the killed were Captain Herman C. Moeller, and Lieutenants William Dieterlie, Ernest Schmidt, and Adam W. Mattice, and among the mortally wounded was Captain Harry E. Breel.

When further efforts to carry the enemies' works by assault were deemed fruitless, the Union forces moved out of their trenches, and crossing the Peninsula and James River, came on the 16th upon the enemy in front of Petersburg. He was soon driven from a strong line of fortifications, extending along a bluff, which stretches away some miles to the south and east of the city. After several days of severe fighting, a line was established some distance in advance of the bluff, where strong lines of entrenchments and covered ways were built. The Eighteenth Corps was posted on the extreme right of the line, its right resting on the Appomattox, and fronting the rebel work known as Fort Clifton. The rebel guns at the fort, and the guns of batteries placed on the opposite side of the river, were so posted as to easily command the position occupied by the regiment, which would have been untenable, had it not been in a measure protected by the Union guns. In this position the regiment remained nearly two months, and during that time, lost eighty in killed and wounded, and a much larger number by disease. Lieutenants Charles Stark, and George B. Sherbon, were among the killed. The latter had just been promoted, but had not been mustered, when, by a sharpshooter's bullet, he was cut down.

On the 5th of July, company F, which, since the 16th of May had been on detached service at Drury's Bluff, re-joined the regiment with full ranks, materially adding to its strength. On the 27th of August, the Eighteenth Corps was relieved by the Tenth Corps, the Eighteenth proceeding to occupy a position on the Bermuda Front, which the Tenth had vacated. On entering the works, the troops were saluted with a fierce fire from the enemy's guns; but this was soon silenced, and they remained in comparative quiet and security to near the close of September. On the night of the 28th, the entire corps was relieved and moving silently, crossed the James on a muffled pontoon bridge, at Aiken's

Landing, and just at day-break, commenced a cautious advance upon the enemy. His pickets were soon encountered and driven, and pushing on at quick time, through a thick wood with tangled undergrowth, the troops at length emerged upon open ground in front of, the rebel works, but a few hundred yards away. Fort Harrison, strongly built and bristling with cannon, was in their immediate front, and before the garrison was hardly aroused, the order to charge at double-quick was given. A long stretch of open ground was passed at a run, and though the enemy brought all his guns and his small arms to bear, he failed to get the range of the advancing troops, firing for the most part too high. At a point within fifty yards of the fort was a slight ravine, which stretched along in its front, capable of affording some protection, and here the line was re-formed, and the men took breath. They were now under a desperate fire, and to go forward was sure to entail heavy slaughter; but pausing only for a moment, the word was again given to charge; and without flinching, as one man the line sprang forward. A terrible volley swept it, and many brave men fell. For an instant it seemed to waver; but only for an instant, and recovering, it dashed on, and the works were, carried. Fortunately, the men of the One Hundred and Eighty-eighth were' well schooled in the use of the Fortress guns, and instantly turned the guns of the fort upon the foe. The victory was complete. The rebel stronghold with all its guns, small arms, and many prisoners, was taken. General Ord; in command of the corps, and General Stannard, in command of the division; were wounded, and General Burnham was killed. The First Division was soon rallied, and advanced upon Fort Gilmer, to the left, under cover of rebel gunboats on the James, and batteries posted along its banks; but it was repulsed, and suffered grievous slaughter in returning to the fort, Lieutenant George M'Neil receiving a mortal wound when close upon the rebel works. At nightfall, the troops were put to work in preparing the fort for effective defense and at dawn it had been reversed and presented a new face. This labor was completed not a moment too soon, for during the night the rebels had been reinforced, and daylight showed them preparing for an assault. They were soon discovered in motion. On they came in Solid column; not a shot was fired film the fort until they had come within a few yards, when, just as they were commencing to utter that unearthly screech, so familiar to Union cars, the signal was given, and such a volley was poured into their ranks as caused them to recoil, and retire in utter confusion, leaving the ground covered with their dead, and their fallen colors. Reforming again they advanced, but again were they stricken and sent staggering back. In desperation, their officers flew to the front, and a third time led them on but all to no purpose. They fell like grain before the sickle of the reaper, and they were finally compelled to yield the ground, and give up the contest. Many of their men were swept in as prisoners, and twenty standards of colors were taken.

Though foiled in their main purpose, they succeeded in throwing a body of sharpshooters upon the right of the Union line, in such a position as to enfilade the brigade line, which began to suffer severely, the traverses of the works having been only partially completed. Captain Henry B. Dickson, who had led the regiment in all this fierce fighting, a gallant officer, was instantly killed by the missile of a sharpshooter, from this enfilading fire. The slaughter in the regiment was very great, the killed amounting to nearly sixty, and the wounded to upwards of a hundred. Lieutenant John Carson was also among the killed.

Not long afterwards, important changes were made in the strength and organization of the corps, and its designation was changed to that of tile Twenty-fourth, the brigade to which the One hundred and Eighty-eighth belonged, being changed to the Third, of the Third Division. Recruits, to the number of four hundred, were sent to the regiment while here. They had been recruited for the Third Artillery, but as that regiment was full, were sent to this. As the cold weather approached, the Brigade, which had been posted some distance to the rear of the fort, as a reserve, erected permanent winter-quarters, the various regiments vying with each other in the plan and finish of their soldier villages.

The monotony of camp life, which was little disturbed during the winter, was broken on the 4th of March 1865. On that day the brigade moved, under Colonel Roberts, to Deep Bottom, and thence proceeded by transports, down the James and up the Rappahannock to Fredericksburg, landing at various points on the way, and effecting immense destruction of stores and property collected for the use of the rebel army. At Fredericksburg, a large quantity of tobacco, ready to be shipped to the rebel capital and depots of supplies, were committed to the flames. Upon its return, the brigade touched at Fortress Monroe, from which point it conveyed supplies to White House, destined for Sheridan; who was coming in from the Shenandoah Valley, having effected the destruction, on his way, of the James River Canal, and the railroads centering at Richmond.

Early on the morning of the 3d of April, there was an unusual stir in the camps about Fort Harrison, and rumors of strange movements of the enemy in front were circulating. The division, which was now commanded by Colonel Devens, was hastily formed, and, advancing, found the rebel lines deserted. A rapid march towards Richmond was commenced, and on coming in sight of the city, it was discovered to be on fire, and the wildest confusion prevailing, the explosion of shells and of whole magazines of ammunition, multiplying the terrors of the burning city. A part of the division was hurried away to assist in checking the flames, which were finally subdued, and comparative quiet was restored. The brigade was soon after settled in camp, in Manchester, a village on the opposite side of the James to Richmond. On the 28th of June, the members of the One Hundred and Ninety-ninth, whose term of service had not expired, were consolidated with those of the One Hundred and Eighty-eighth, with James C. Briscoe, of the former, as Colonel, and S. Irvin Givin, of the latter, as Lieutenant Colonel, and the new regiment was ordered to Lynchburg. Soon after arriving there, Colonel Briscoe was promoted to Brigadier General, and placed in command of the post, leaving the regiment in command of Lieutenant Colonel Given, who retained it until the final muster out. Five of the companies were sent out into as many different counties surrounding the post, for guard and provost duty, and the remaining five were sent to Danvine, where they were also distributed for similar duty. Thus separated, the companies served until the 14th of December, when they were ordered to assemble at City Point, where they were mustered out of service

The 188th Pennsylvania Volunteers, once organized, was assigned to the First Division, Eighteenth Corps, Army of the James. The organization of the Eighteenth Army Corps was under Major General William F. Smith. The officers of the two echelons below the First Division of the 18th Army Corps follow:

First Division Brig. General William T.H. Brooks

First Brigade Brig. General Gilman Marston

- 81st N.Y. Colonel Jacob J. De Forest
- 95th N.Y. Colonel Edgar M. Cullen
- 98th N.Y. Colonel Frederick F. Wead
- 139th N.Y. Colonel Samuel H. Roberts

Second Brigade Brig. General Hiram Burnham

- 8th Conn. Colonel John E. Ward
- 10th N.H. Lieut. Colonel John Coughlin
- 13th N.H. Colonel Aaron F. Stevens
- 118th N.Y. Colonel Oliver Keese, Jr.

Third Brigade Colonel Horace T. Sanders

- 92nd N.Y. Lieut. Colonel Hiram Anderson, Jr.
- 58th Pa. Lieut. Colonel Montgomery Martin

- 188th Pa. Lieut. Colonel George K. Bowen
- 19th Wis. Lieut. Colonel Rollin M. Strong

Artillery Brigade Major Theodore H. Schenck

- 4th Wis. Captain George B. Easterly L
- 4th U.S. Lieutenant John S. Hunt A
- 5th U.S. Lieutenant Charles P. Muh

Some other 188th PA Vols facts follow:

- Enrollment: 1,200 Officers and Men. "Recruits" filled the remaining ranks.
- Casualties:
    - Killed or died from wounds: 10 Officers; 114 Men.
    - Died from disease: 2 Officers; 66 men
- The unit mustered out, at City Point VA, on 14 December 1865.
- The Casemate Museum at Ft. Monroe has a photo of the band of the 3rd PA Hvy Arty (152d Pa Vols-) mustered on the Ft. Monroe parade grounds.
- The 188th Regiment Flag is preserved at the Pennsylvania State Archives, located in Harrisburg PA.
- Battles:
    - Drewry's Bluff
    - Cold Harbor
    - Petersburg
    - Chaffin's Farm
    - Fair Oaks (second)
    - Occupation of Richmond

Further information about the 188th Pennsylvania Volunteers is found in Samuel Bates writing from 1898 as follows.

From the Book by Samuel P. Bates

ONE HUNDRED AND EIGHTY-EIGHTH REGIMENT.

THE Third Artillery, One Hundred and Fifty-second of the line, was organized for garrison duty at Fortress Monroe. Numerous recruits were sent to it from time to time, after entering the service, and as it sustained few losses, its ranks were not only kept full, but a large number of unassigned men accumulated. The number of surplus men had become so great by the first of April, 1864, that an order was issued from the War Department, directing a call to be made for volunteers from this regiment, to form a new infantry regiment. In response to the call, over six hundred men volunteered, and in less than two weeks, a new regiment, afterwards known as the One Hundred and Eighty-eighth, was organized, with nearly nine hundred men. The following field officers were appointed, promoted from captains of companies in the Third: George K. Bowen, Lieutenant Colonel; Francis H. Reichard, Major. A large proportion of the men had served in other organizations before entering the Third, over three hundred having been in the Reserve Corps. The organization, arming, and equipping of the new regiment had scarcely been completed, when it was ordered to the field. On the morning of April 25th, it took up the line of march from Camp Hamilton, a mile and a half from the Fortress, where the organization had been made, for Yorktown. Upon its arrival, it was assigned to the Third Brigade, First Division, of the Eighteenth Corps, where it was associated with the Second Connecticut, Fourth New Hampshire, and Fifty-eighth Pennsylvania regiments.

On the 4th of May, the Eighteenth Corps moved by transports to Bermuda Hundred, above City Point, on the James. Skirmishing commenced soon after the debarkation, which continued for a full week before the advance reached Fort Darling, at Drury's Bluff, a strong work upon a commanding position. At Proctor's Creek, on the 10th, the command was warmly engaged, losing two killed, and on the 13th and 14th, again sustained some loss. Major Reichard, who was in command of the skirmish line of the brigade, had succeeded in driving the enemy out of a small redoubt, within eight hundred yards of the fort, and had posted some of his men behind some log huts, where they picked off the enemy's gunners. During Sunday, comparative quiet prevailed, the men busying themselves in throwing up breast-works. On the morning of Monday the 16th, the enemy having massed his forces and prepared them for action, under cover of a dense fog, which hung like an impenetrable curtain on every hand, made an unexpected and most determined assault. The firing was of necessity much at random, but the struggle was maintained with unflinching valor, and positions were taken and re-taken at the point of the bayonet. The enemy bore heavily upon the right of the line, and Heckman's Brigade, which held this ground, was driven in. The Third Brigade was moved to its support, and in the midst of the movement, the right wing of the regiment, consisting of six companies, under command of Colonel Bowen, by order of Captain Reed, of General Brooks' staff, was separated from the left, and took position to the right, and considerably in advance of the rest of the brigade. Soon after taking position, Captain Reed rode forward and informed Colonel Bowen that the position was an important one, and must be held to the last extremity. Other aids came, and finally General Brooks himself, to encourage the men, and to magnify the importance of the position. Finally, Captain Reed called for volunteers to go forward a few hundred yards to bring off a Union battery which had been abandoned. The battalion responded in a body, and soon had possession of the battery, but found it so disabled, that they were unable to remove it. Discovering this movement, the enemy opened a heavy and a most murderous fire upon the command, compelling it to fall back to its first position. By this fire, Captain Hiram R. Shinkle was mortally wounded, and fell into the enemy's hands, dying while a prisoner at Richmond. As the command executed this retrograde movement, the portion of the Union line, which was posted in its rear, unfortunately mistook it for a charge of the enemy, and opened fire upon it, delivering two volleys before the mistake was discovered. The division was finally driven back, and took position behind its works at Bermuda Hundred. The loss in this unfortunate engagement, was eleven killed and sixty wounded. The command was immediately put to fortifying, and for a period of two weeks, it was kept busy in strengthening and improving the works.

Near the close of May, the Eighteenth Corps, under command of General Baldy Smith, was ordered to reinforce the army of the Potomac, and on the evening of the 1st of June, came up to the Sixth Corps near Cold Harbor, taking position on its right. Scarcely had the newly arrived forces got into position, when the word to advance was quietly passed along the lines, and a simultaneous and most desperate charge, by the entire Union force in position, was made on the enemy's strong lines of well abatised earth-works and forts. These proved to be well manned, and the storm of deadly missiles which was poured upon the advancing troops, caused them to recoil. Three times the lines were rallied, and returned to the attack, when, just as darkness was setting in, the enemy's outer line of works was carried, and though exposed until far into the night to a desperate artillery fire, was held and fortified, every spade, pick, tin cup, plate, even to the hands of the men, being brought into requisition. At a little before dawn, on the morning of the 3d, the troops were again formed, and two desperate charges were made, but all with no avail. Their ranks were swept with terrible effect, and they were compelled to desist, after having displayed unparalleled daring and courage, and left the ground strewn with their dead and wounded, many of them lying close up under the enemy's guns. Falling back to their lines, they fell to fortifying and strengthening their works, and for a period of ten days, artillery was plied with little cessation, but without material effect. In the two brief struggles on the 1st and 3d, the One Hundred and Eighty-eighth lost twenty-four killed, and a large number wounded. Among the killed were Captain Herman C. Moeller, and Lieutenants William Dieterlie, Ernest Schmidt, and Adam W. Mattice, and among the mortally wounded was Captain Harry E. Breel.

When further efforts to carry the enemy's works by assault were deemed fruitless, the Union forces moved out of their trenches, and crossing the Peninsula and James River, came on the 16th upon the enemy in front of Petersburg. He was soon driven from a strong line of fortifications, extending along a bluff which stretches away some miles to the south and east of the city. After several days of severe fighting, a line was established some distance in advance of the bluff, where strong lines of intrenchments and covered ways were built. The Eighteenth Corps was posted on the extreme right of the line, its right resting on the Appomattox, and fronting the rebel work known as Fort Clifton. The rebel guns at the fort, and the guns of batteries placed on the opposite side of the river, were so posted as to easily command the position occupied by the regiment, which would have been untenable, had it not been in a measure protected by the Union guns. In this position the regiment remained nearly two months, and during that time, lost eighty in killed and wounded, and a much larger number by disease. Lieutenants Charles Stark, and George B. Sherbon, were among the killed. The latter had just been promoted, but had not been mustered, when, by a sharp-shooter's bullet, he was cut down.

On the 5th of July, company F, which, since the 16th of May had been on detached service at Drury's Bluff, re-joined the regiment with full ranks, materially adding to its strength. On the 27th of August, the Eighteenth Corps was relieved by the Tenth Corps, the Eighteenth proceeding to occupy a position on the Bermuda Front, which the Tenth had vacated. On entering the works, the troops were saluted with a fierce fire from the enemy's guns; but this was soon silenced, and they remained in comparative quiet and security to near the close of September. On the night of the 28th, the entire corps was relieved, and moving silently, crossed the James on a muffled pontoon bridge, at Aiken's Landing, and just at day-break, commenced a cautious advance upon the enemy. His pickets were soon encountered and driven, and pushing on at quick time, through a thick wood with tangled undergrowth, the troops at length emerged upon open ground in front of the rebel works, but a few hundred yards away. Fort Harrison, strongly built and bristling with cannon, was in their immediate front, and before the garrison was hardly aroused, the order to charge at double-quick was given. A long stretch of open ground was passed at a run, and though the enemy brought all his guns and his small arms to bear, he failed to get the range of the advancing troops, firing for the most part too high. At a point within fifty yards of the fort was a slight ravine, which stretched along in its front, capable of affording some protection, and here the line was re-formed, and the men took breath. They were now under a desperate fire, and to go forward was sure to entail heavy slaughter; but pausing only for a moment, the word was again given to charge, and without flinching, as one man the line sprang forward. A terrible volley swept it, and many brave men fell. For an instant it seemed to waver; but only for an instant, and recovering, it dashed on, and the works were carried. Fortunately, the men of the One Hundred and Eighty-eighth were well schooled in the use of the Fortress guns, and instantly turned the guns of the fort upon the foe. The victory was complete. The rebel stronghold, with all its guns, small arms, and many prisoners, was taken. General Ord, in command of the corps, and General Stannard, in command of the division, were wounded, and General Burnham was killed. The First Division was soon rallied, and advanced upon Fort Gilmer, to the left, under cover of rebel gunboats on the James, and batteries posted along its banks; but it was repulsed, and suffered grievous slaughter in returning to the fort, Lieutenant George M'Neil receiving a mortal wound when close upon the rebel works. At night-fall, the troops were put to work in preparing the fort for effective defense, and at dawn it had been reversed and presented a new face. This labor was completed not a moment too soon, for during the night the rebels had been reinforced, and daylight showed them preparing for an assault. They were soon discovered in motion. On they came in solid column; but not a shot was fired from the fort until they had come within a few yards, when, just as they were commencing to utter that unearthly screech, so familiar to Union ears, the signal was given, and such a volley was poured into their ranks as caused them to recoil, and retire in utter confusion, leaving the ground covered with their dead, and their fallen colors. Re-forming, again they advanced, but again were they stricken, and sent staggering back. In desperation, their officers flew to the front, and a third time led them on; but all to no purpose. They fell like grain before the sickle of the reaper, and they were finally compelled to yield the ground, and give up the contest. Many of their men were swept in as prisoners, and twenty stands of colors taken.

Though foiled in their main purpose, they succeeded in throwing a body of sharp-shooters upon the right of the Union line, in such a position as to enfilade the brigade line, which began to suffer severely, the traverses of the works having been only partially completed. Captain Henry B. Dickson, who had led the regiment in all this fierce fighting, a gallant officer, was instantly killed by the missile of a sharp-shooter, from this enfilading fire. The slaughter in the regiment was very great, the killed amounting to nearly sixty, and the wounded to upwards of a hundred. Lieutenant John Carson was also among the killed.

Not long afterwards, important changes were made in the strength and organization of the corps, and its designation was changed to that of the Twenty-fourth, the brigade to which the One Hundred and Eighty-eighth belonged, being changed to the Third, of the Third Division. Recruits, to the number of four hundred, were sent to the regiment while here. They had been recruited for the Third Artillery, but as that regiment was full, were sent to this. As the cold weather approached, the Brigade, which had been posted some distance to the rear of the fort, as a reserve, erected permanent winter-quarters, the various regiments vieing with each other in the plan and finish of their soldier villages.

The monotony of camp life, which was little disturbed during the winter, was broken on the 4th of March, 1865. On that day the brigade moved, under Colonel Roberts, to Deep Bottom, and thence proceeded by transports, down the James and up the Rappahannock to Fredericksburg, landing at various points on the way, and effecting immense destruction of stores and property collected for the use of the rebel army. At Fredericksburg, a large quantity of tobacco, ready to be shipped to the rebel capital and depots of supplies, were committed to the flames. Upon its return, the brigade touched at Fortress Monroe, from which point it conveyed supplies to White House, destined for Sheridan, who was coming in from the Shenandoah Valley, having effected the destruction, on his way, of the James River Canal, and the railroads centring at Richmond.

ONE HUNDRED AND EIGHTY-EIGHTH REGIMENT,

Early on the morning of the 3d of April, there was an unusual stir in the camps about Fort Harrison, and rumors of strange movements of the enemy in front were circulating. The division, which was now commanded by Colonel Devens, was hastily formed, and, advancing, found the rebel lines deserted. A rapid march towards Richmond was commenced, and on coming in sight of the city, it was discovered to be on fire, and the wildest confusion prevailing, the explosion of shells and of whole magazines of ammunition, multiplying the terrors of the burning city. A part of the division was hurried away to assist in checking the flames, which were finally subdued, and comparative quiet was restored. The brigade was soon after settled in camp, in Manchester, a village on the opposite side of the James to Richmond. On the 28th of June, the members of the One Hundred and Ninety-ninth, whose term of service had not expired, were consolidated with those of the One Hundred and Eighty-eighth, with James C. Briscoe, of the former, as Colonel, and S. Irvin Givin, of the latter, as Lieutenant Colonel, and the new regiment was ordered to Lynchburg. Soon after arriving there, Colonel Briscoe was promoted to Brigadier General, and placed in command of the post, leaving the regiment in command of Lieutenant Colonel Given, who retained it until the final muster out. Five of the companies were sent out into as many different counties surrounding the post, for guard and provost duty, and the remaining five were sent to Danville, where they were also distributed for similar duty. Thus separated, the companies served until the 14th of December, when they were ordered to assemble at City Point, where they were mustered out of service.

FIELD AND STAFF OFFICERS.

NAME.	RANK.	DATE OF MUSTER INTO SERVICE.	REMARKS.
James C. Briscoe	Colonel	Oct. 3, '64,	Transferred from 199th regiment Pennsylvania Volunteers, June 28, 1865—discharged Dec. 14, 1865.
George K. Bowen	Lt. Col.	Nov. 13, '62,	Promoted from Capt. battery C, 152d regiment P. V., April 29, 1864—commissioned Colonel, April 12, 1864—not mustered—dis. March 27, 1865.
John G. Gregg	do	Sept. 16, '62,	Promoted from Capt. Co. D to Major, Jan. 19, 1865—to Lieut. Colonel, April 18, 1865—com. Colonel, May 1, 1865—not mus.—resigned July 1, 1865.
S. Irvin Given	do	Sept. 23, '62,	Promoted from Captain company K, July 2, 1865—commissioned Colonel, November 26, 1865—not mus.—mustered out with regiment, Dec. 14, 1865.
Francis H. Reichard	Major	Feb. 10, '63,	Promoted from Captain company M, 152d regiment P. V., April 1, 1864—commissioned Lieut. Colonel, July 1, 1864—not mustered—wounded at Cold Harbor, Va., June 4, 1864—resigned Jan. 17, 1865.
Matthew Keck	Adj.	Dec. 22, '63,	Promoted from Quartermaster Sergeant battery E, 152d reg. P. V., April 6, 1864—dis. June 4, 1864.
Henry B. Dickson	do	Sept. 15, '62,	Promoted from 2d Lt. battery E, 152d reg. P. V., to Adjt., April 1, 1864—to Capt. Co. F, April 10, 1864.
Byron F. Davis	do	Jan. 19, '63,	Promoted from 1st Lieutenant Co. C, Sept. 13, 1864—mustered out with regiment, Dec. 14, 1865.
Theodore Spangler	Q. M.	Oct. 29, '62,	Promoted from 2d Lt. battery M, 152d reg. P. V., April 1, 1864—discharged by S. O., Sept. 12, 1864.
Henry C. Wood	do	April 6, '64,	Pr. fr. 1st Lt. Co. A, Sept. 13, '64—to Capt. 117th reg. U. S. C. T., Dec. 8, 1864—resigned Aug. 16, 1865.

Members of Company F

188th Pennsylvania Volunteers

Name	Co.	Rank In	Rank Out	Also Know As
Adams, Henry	F	Private	Private	
Anderson, John	F	Private	Private	
Atkinson, Louis E.	F&S	Surgeon	Surgeon	
Augestine, Peter S.	F&B	Private	Private	
Austin, John	F	First Sergeant	First Lieutenant	
Axton, Matthew C.	F&E	Private	Private	
Bartow, Thomas	F	Private	Corporal	
Baumherst, Herman	F&S	Hospital Steward	Hospital Steward	Baumhorst
Baxter, Francis	F	Private	Private	
Beers, Lewis R.	F	Corporal	Corporal	
Blain, George A.	F	Private	Private	
Bohart, John	F	Private	Private	
Bowen, George K.	F&S	Lieutenant Colonel	Lieutenant Colonel	
Brees, Evan	F	Private	Private	
Brewington, Joshua	F	Private	Private	Brewington, Joseph
Briscoe, Joseph C.	F&S	Colonel	Colonel	
Brown, Alonzo F.	F	Private	Private	Brown, Alonzo T.
Brown, Edward	F	Private	Private	
Bruington, Joshua	F	Private	Private	
Bryner, Samuel	F	Private	Private	
Buckley, Curnell	F	Private	Private	
Campbell, John	F	Private	Private	
Cannon, George W.	F	Private	Private	Canon
Chase, Milton B.	F	Private	Private	
Christy, Samuel H.	F	Private	Private	
Clemmings, Francis	F	Private	Private	
Collison, Amos	F	Private	Private	Cullison
Collison, Kinsey	F	Private	Private	Cullison
Collison, Theodore	F	Private	Private	Cullison
Conkel, William	F	Private	Private	
Coppridge, Joel A.	F	Private	Private	
Crahan, Martin	F	Corporal	Sergeant	Crayon, Creahan
Crawford, John	F	Private	Private	
Custer, John	F	Private	Private	
Davis, Byron	F&C	Private	Adjutant	
Decker, Benjamin	F	Private	Private	
Delany, John	F	Private	Private	
Dial, Abraham S.	F&E	First Lieutenant	Captain	
Dial, John W.	F	Private	Corporal	
Dickens, William	F	Private	Private	
Dickson, Henry B.	F	Captain	Captain	
Dixon, John	F	Corporal	Corporal	Donoldson

Name	Co.	Rank In	Rank Out	Also Know As
Donaldson, Henry	F	Private	Private	Donalson
Donhoe, Patrick	F	Private	Private	Donohoe
Donty, Cyrus	F	Private	Private	Doubty, Dowty
Name	Co.	Rank In	Rank Out	Also Know As
Doulin, Elijah	F	Private	Private	Dowlin
Eckhart, Samuel	F	Private	Private	
Eichel, John X.	F	Private	Private	
Elliot, Joseph	F&S	Sergeant	Captain	
Evans, Samuel D.	F	Private	Private	
Feinour, Joseph	F	Private	Private	
Firestone, Simon	F	Private	Private	
Fitterer, Peter	F	Private	Private	
Fry, George W.	F	Private	Private	
Gallagher, Charles	F	Private	Private	
Gallagher, Dennis	F	Private	Private	
Garland, John K.	F	Private	Private	
Geiser, Anthony	F	Wagoner	Corporal	
Gensel, Joseph	F	Private	Private	
Gibbons, Ambrose	F	Private	Private	
Gilbaugh, Valentine	F	Private	Private	
Gilson, David A.	F	Private	Private	
Grider, Jacob	F	Private	Private	
Griffin, David	F	Private	Private	
Griffin, Lewis	F	Private	Private	
Hague, John	F	Private	Private	
Haines, Samuel O.	F	Private	Private	
Hall, Frank	F	Private	Private	
Hamilton, George	F	Private	Private	
Hammerley, G. Wharton	F&S	First Lieutenant	First Lieutenant / Quarter Master	
Hankey, John	F	Private	Corporal	Hanky
Harety, Edward	F	Private	Private	Harraty, Harrety, Harriety
Harris, Samuel O.	F	Private	Private	
Harrison, David B.F.	F	Private	Private	
Haumhorst, Hermann	F&S	Hospital Steward	Hospital Steward	
Hawk, Philip	F&S	Chaplain	Chaplain	
Hawksey, John	F	Private	Corporal	
Heinbaugh, Henry	F&B	Private	Private	Hinebah, also first name Jacob
Hileman, William	F	Private	Private	
Holland, Springer	F	Private	Private	
Hulee, Charles E.	F&I	Private	Private	Hulse
Israel, William	F	Corporal	Corporal	
Jackson, William A.	F	Private	Private	
Jeffers, James H.	F	Sergeant	Private	
Jennings, Andrew	F	Private	Private	
Johnson, William B.	F	Corporal	Private	
Joyce, Michael J.	F	Private	Sergeant Major	

Name	Co.	Rank In	Rank Out	Also Know As
Keck, Matthew	F&S	First Lieutenant	Adjutant	Kecke
Keel, Henry	F	Private	Private	
Kelly, Matthew	F	Private	Private	
Keppner, Isaac	F&S	Private	Commissary Sergeant	
Kern, Francis I.	F&S	Surgeon	Surgeon	
Keystner, Andrew	F	Private	Private	Kinstner, Kistner, Knistner
Kindy, Henry D.	F	Private	Private	
Kinsley, George	F	Private	Private	
Name	Co.	Rank In	Rank Out	Also Know As
Kinsley, William H.	F	Private	Private	
Koerner, William H.	F	Private	Private	
Leech, Lott C.	F&S	Commissary Sergeant	Regimental Quarter Master	also under Lott I.
Leighton, Walter H.	F&S	Assistant Surgeon	Assistant Surgeon	
Lindsey, Andrew	F	Private	Private	
Lindsey, William	F	Private	Private	
Loveland, George W.	F	Private	Private	
Lowrey, Samuel	F	Private	Private	
Lush, Theodore	F	Private	Private	
Mackey, John	F	Private	Private	
Mallon, John	F	Private	Private	
Maloney, Andrew	F	Private	Private	
McAndrews, Patrick	F	Private	Private	
McCluen, Edward L.	F	Sergeant	First Lieutenant	
McEwen, Peter	F	Private	Corporal	
McGlathery, Joseph	F	Private	Private	McGlethery
McGlaughlin, John	F	Private	Private	McLaughlin
McMahon, James	F	Private	Private	
McMichael, Albert	F	Private	Private	
McMichael, Lemuel	F	Private	Private	
McNeil, George	F	First Lieutenant	First Lieutenant	McNeal, McNiel
Meitzer, Abraham	F	Private	Private	Metzler
Miller, Abraham	F	Private	Private	Also under Abram
Miller, Clinton A.	F&B	Private	Private	
Miller, William E.	F	Private	Private	
Mills, Allen	F	Private	Private	
Milroy, Michael H.	F	Private	Private	
Montgomery, Samuel	F	Private	Private	
Moore, William	F	Corporal	Sergeant	
Mund, Henry	F&S	Quarter Master Sergeant	Quarter Master Sergeant	
Myers, George	F	Private	Private	
Nicalo, Aaron	F	Private	Private	Nicola
Noll, Jacob	F&B	Private	Private	
O'Brian, John	F	Private	Private	O'Brien
O'Donnell, Morris	F	Private	Private	
Orr, John W.	F	Private	Private	
Palmer, John	F	Private	Private	
Perry, Joseph	F	Private	Private	
Pidgeon, James	F	Private	Private	

Name		Rank In	Rank Out	Notes
Pitt, Joseph	F	Private	Private	
Potter, Harry	F	Sergeant	Sergeant	Also under Harvey
Potter, Joseph K.	F	Private	Corporal	
Quinn, William	F	Private	Private	
Rager, Jacob	F&B	Private	Private	Reazer, Reger
Reichard, Francis H.	F&S	Major	Lieutenant Colonel	
Reinboth, Henry B.	F	Second Lieutenant	Captain	
Rennard, Benjamin	F	Private	Private	
Rhile, John	F	Private	Private	
Robertson, Anthony	F	Private	Private	
Robinson, John	F	Private	Private	
Rogers, James	F	Private	Private	
Rough, Jacob	F	Private	Private	
Russell, John	F	Private	Private	
Ryan, John	F	Private	Private	
Salmon, Michael	F	Private	Private	
Sands, George	F	Private	Private	
Sarber, William	F&B	Private	Private	Sorber
Schultz, Edward	F	Private	Private	Shultz
Scott, Abner F.	F	Musician	Musician	Also under Abner V.
Scott, James	F	Private	Private	
Secrist, George	F	Private	Private	Seichrist, Seicrist
Shaner, Jacob	F	Private	Private	
Singles, William H.	F	Private	Private	Also under William N.
Smith, James	F	Private	Private	
Smith, Porter	F	Private	Private	
Smith, Tracy H.	F	Private	Private	
Spengler, Theodore	F&S	Quarter Master	Regimental Quarter Master	
Spout, John	F	Private	Private	Sprout
Spout, George	F	Private	Private	
Steever, John W.	F	Private	Corporal	
Sterner, Ross R.	F	Sergeant	Sergeant	
Stiles, Richard	F&B	Private	Private	
Surber, William	F&R	Private	Private	
Swartz, August	F	Private	Private	Swertz
Vanleer, George A	F	Private	Private	Also under George W.
Vincent, Levi	F	Private	Private	Vinson
Walch, Edward	F	Private	Private	Welch, Welsh
Walter, William Harvey	F	Corporal	Sergeant	Walters (*incorrect*)
Ward, John	F	Private	Private	Warde
Watson, Luke	F	Private	Corporal	
Weise, Francis	F	Private	Private	
Welsh, James	F	Private	Private	
Welsh, Michael	F	Private	Private	
Welsh, William	F	Private	Private	
Wertman, James	F	Private	Private	
Whitten, John T.	F	Private	Private	
Whitter, George	F	Private	Private	

Williams, Harry	F	Private	Corporal	
Williams, Henry	F	Private	Private	
Williamson, Lewis	F	Sergeant	Sergeant	
Wise, Francis	F	Private	Private	
Wood, Henry C.	F&S	First Lieutenant	First Lieutenant	
Workman, James	F	Private	Private	
Zimmerman, William	F	Musician	Musician	

William Harvey Walter, Civilian Again

William returned home to Christiana Hundred, New Castle County, Delaware, on December 16th, 1865 and to his father John H. Walter, and the family owned a mill along the Brandywine Creek. John and his second wife, Elizabeth had four younger children to rear: Granville W., Edward, Abigail (Abbe) J., and Mary.

It was not long until William made his way to Philadelphia looking for work. As you have read from his diary, the idea was to find a clerking position and he applied to the Philadelphia Custom House. This proving fruitless, William finally turned to the vocation that he had learned since a lad. And so, William went to work for the Media Mills, Media, Pennsylvania on March 1st, 1867.

All during this time William continued to correspond with Rosanna Kirk of Upper Providence, Pa. Rosanna's father, John Kirk was a farmer in the district and they had met at the home of friends in nearby Media.

William and Rosanna were married in Philadelphia, Pa., February 25, 1869 and soon after the young couple settled near Media but soon moved to London Grove, Pa. Three sons and a daughter joined the family. Lewis Kirk Walter, named for Rosanna's brother was born in 1871, Sharpless Walter, named in honor of Walter's cousin, born 1874, Townsend H. Walter, named in honor of William's brother, born 1878 and Florence Sidney Walter, born 1880.

From the beginning William was active with the Grand Army of the Republic veterans, joining Courtland Saunders Post #21 in West Philadelphia, at that time located at 39th St. above Market St. While a member of Post #21 William enjoyed the various events that were held. He attended as many outings as he could, at first with his wife, Rosanna (Rosie) Kirk Walter and upon her passing, his daughter, Florence Walter Reynolds. He was elected Post Commander and enjoyed all the trappings that that exalted title gave him.

Post Commanders in the G.A.R wore this ribbon.

Later after Post 21 dissolved due to dwindling numbers of veterans, William joined Post #2 on 12th & Wallace in Philadelphia, the longest lasting of all the G.A.R. posts. Today, the G.A.R. museum is housed in this building and can be visited.

William continued to be active right up to the time of his death in October 1936. He attended the wedding of his granddaughter, Florence Hopkins Reynolds to Richard Wesley Stewart on June 20th,

1936 and it was said that he complained loudly that the festivities ended too early for his liking. It is from this union that I come and it is with sadness that I never got to know William Harvey Walter or his beloved wife. However, I do feel that as I have transcribed his words, researched the names and places mentioned in his diary I have come to know this great grandfather better. William's watch and Rosanna's portrait continue to have a place of honor in our home although now far removed from Pennsylvania and the United States.

"Last Call Men"

William Harvey Walter was irritated at the expression "Last Call Men" a derogatory term applied to soldiers who served only in the last year of the war. A proud and active member of the G.A.R., William contributed the following letter to the editor of the *National Tribune* of October 8th, 1892, in which he attempts to set the historical record straight regarding his regiment's short term of service. The original article entitled "Last Call Big Bounty Men" appeared in a prior issue of the paper.

Last Call Men

A Pennsylvania Comrade who is Not Ashamed to be called a '64 Man.

EDITOR, *NATIONAL TRIBUNE*: The article in your last issue under the head of "Last call, big bounty men" I have read with great interest more especially, I suppose, for the reason that I served in one of the regiments which you note; but as the article in question would seem to give the impression that we were a one year's regiment I desire to correct that error. The members of this regiment to which I allude (the 188th Pa.) were all three years' men and had already been in the service from periods ranging from 1862 down to within a month of the formation of the regiment at Camp Hamilton in the Spring of 1864. It was raised from the 3rd Pa. Art., then garrisoning Fort Monroe, by a special order from the War Department, obtained by Gen. Butler, and we enjoyed the unique distinction of being the only Pennsylvania regiment raised on rebel soil, while a large percent was composed of men who had already served nearly two years in the mother regiment. Another large percent were those who had served in other organizations and had either been discharged for wounds received or by expiration of term of service, but had enlisted prior to the offering of the big bounty; therefore, a very small percentage of them received a big bounty, and these were not all new men unused to war by any manner of means. Nine out of every 10, it is safe to say, had seen service, and severe service too; and while we were a new organization as infantry it was a veteran regiment in every sense of the word. It was more than could be said of any other regiment in the field. Batteries of artillery could have been manned by officers and men from its ranks and served with the same precision as the best of them. Every battlefield of the Eastern armies was represented, so it is not strange that when that great campaign opened that was to task human endurance to its utmost that we were always placed in the advance. I think I speak the sentiment of the survivors when I say we are not ashamed of our record even if we are classed with the "Last call big bounty men." – W. H. Walter, 188th Pa, West Grove, Pa.

I wish to thank Edward Worman of Whitesville, New York, for bringing this article to my attention. - *Carol-Lynn Sappé*

The Harvey/Walter Family

Search for a Family

William Harvey Walter's obituary left tantalizing clues as to his genealogical background. It stated that Mr. Walter was a Quaker and a descendant of John Walter, who came to America with William Penn settling on the Brandywine and on the maternal side, he was a descendant of Mary Harvey, a daughter of William Harvey, who settled at Chadds Ford in 1712.

The computer is a great tool when doing family research. Many web sites are available where you just plug in the name and, instant family. Well, then again, maybe not.

Not knowing the names of William's parents the search did not get very far. Add the name William Walter and even William Harvey Walter as very common in Chester and Delaware counties of Pennsylvania the research began to bog down. Not to be deterred, I plug in the name Townsend Walter, which should do the trick. Oh so wrong again. There were as many Townsend's as there were William's. And trying other family names I had was getting me nowhere fast.

After much frustration and many hours online combing site after site it became clear it was necessary to make the trip to Pennsylvania. So, another year went by before a trip could be arranged.

Fate played a big hand in finding part of my family roots. Thanks to the Chadds Ford Historical Society, I was introduced to a volume of work "History of Chester County, Pennsylvania, Biographical and Genealogical".

Although I did not find William Harvey Walter staring me from the pages of the book I did find a picture of Jacob W. Harvey, footnote 50.

Uncle Jacob W. Harvey, as it turned out, was born 10th month, 1 day, 1826 in Pennsbury Township to Pusey Harvey and his wife Phebe, daughter of John and Hannah Way of Kennett. As with the other Harvey name bearers, his parents were strict Quakers.

Jacob was apprenticed to Isaiah Price, of West Chester where he learned the trade of bricklayer. But Jacob had a thirst for knowledge and while the other apprentices lounged about he read philosophy, history, botany, astronomy, and other topics he found interesting. After completing his apprenticeship he spent his summers as a bricklayer but his winters as a teacher. Then at the age of nineteen he entered the Unionville Academy as a student. Under the tutelage of Jonathan Gause his intellect grew. After completing the Unionville Academy course he entered his trade and spent four years building houses in Philadelphia. In 1855 Jacob accepted the position of principal of the Kennett Square High School and in 1857 was made principal of the Fairville Institute where William Harvey Walter visited him in 1864. During 1877, Dr. Wickersham, State superintendent of public school, appointed Jacob to fill the unexpired term of Chester county superintendent of schools. Jacob Harvey was re-elected to the office in 1878 and again in 1881. The schools under his jurisdiction gained popularity and the number of students increased.

Not bad considering my father always told me my family was just three generations out of the trees! Take that dad; one of our chimps was a local educator!

Unfortunately, the Chadds Ford Historical Society could not provide further information as to whom were William's parents and without them my search would end. They did, however, know where my next stop should be, the Chester County Historical Society.

The society librarian knew everything there was to find in "her" library. She was so well versed in the subject she is a walking encyclopedia of Chester county history.
The wealth of information stored within the historic building is enormous. We started with the card index where every family who lived in the county was cross-filed. From there we moved to the obituary collection that had been carefully hand done by volunteers since the early 20th century. The library also contains genealogical information done by earlier generations and is a treasure trove of information on the Society of Friends.

We found Townsend H. Walter in the obituary collection. The obituary listed William Harvey Walter as surviving brother along with the names of their father and mother: John and Elizabeth Jane Walter. A visit to the Old Kennett Meeting burial grounds and I had found my Quaker ancestors.

However, I also discovered a problem. Elizabeth Jane could not be the birth mother of William or Townsend so who was John H. Walter's first wife?

Again turning to web based genealogy soft ware and research I discovered a who's who of Pennsylvania Quaker founding families located in Monthly Meeting records. My search was over.

For those interested in genealogy I have attached William Harvey Walter's lineage.

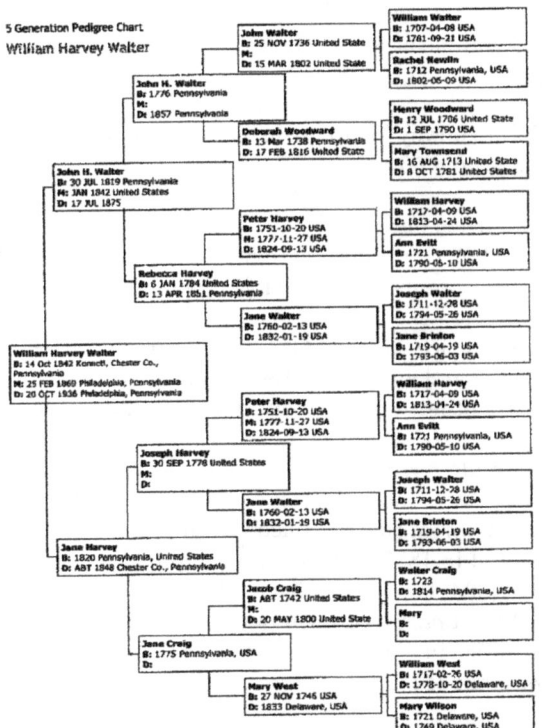

G. D. Vanderveer
and the Steamship Susan

At the time William Harvey Walter served in the 188th Pennsylvania Volunteers a member of my father's ancestors also served the Union forces in his capacity as master of a steamship.

G.D. Vanderveer kept a diary but it did not survive to the present day. What survived is a letter he wrote to his wife and children. It is presented here in honor of his service and that of all steamship masters and crews who served during the war.

The Philadelphia Steam Propeller Company owned the Steamship Susan and its homeport was Philadelphia, Pennsylvania. When the Civil War irrupted, the Quartermaster Department of the War Department conscripted ships and their masters into service. On April 16, 1862, the Susan was renamed the Ironsides and entered into service. Her master was G.D. Vanderveer. The steamship remained in service to the Quartermaster Department until March 21, 1866 at which time the Philadelphia Steam Propeller Companies' ownership was reinstated.

As the Steamship Ironsides, the ship saw service to the Army of the Potomac and James. G.D. Vanderveer sent the following letter to his wife:

Fredericksburg, June 19th, 1865

Dear Wife and Children,

      With the utmost esteem, I address this communication to you informing you that I Arrived at the above named place, some days since, but am about to embrace the first opportunity of writing to you as this is the first Mail that has left this place. Since my arrival at it, there not being but two Mails per week. I did not go to Norfolk as I expected from Fortress Monroe but have at last brought up at this dilapidated City with a Cargo of forage. I thought I had seen much of the ill effects of the war since I have been in the South. But I have been in no City that has suffered like Fredericksburg, it has been quiet a large City that is for a Southern City. But there is not, scarcely a house left in it that has not had a cannon ball through it. And many of them have been layed level with the Earth. There is much destitution here among the inhabitants.

      Dear Family, how I wish I could see you once more. But yet it is imposable for me to say when I shall be permitted that pleasure, as it requires my whole attention here just now. To keep my steamer employed for the Government are lining Steamers up a most every day and should I now leave to come home and the least little thing should occur they would at once lie the Steamer up and I do not wish mine layed up yet if I can possible avoid it, for times I know must be very dull at home just now. But yet I hope if God be willing to be able to make you a visit home sometime next Month.

      I expect to go from here to Washington. And I hope to hear from you on my arrival at that City as I sent to City Point for all letters there for me. I have not learned as yet, who you paid with the money I sent you. But I hope you paid Mr. Dixon, Mr. Hyde and as much more as you had cash to pay with. But I will pay all that you have not paid should God permit me to get my pay from the Government and get home once more. Remember me to my dear little ones, and all inquiring friends.

And now with the sincere hope that God may bless you and permit you to enjoy good health as this now leaves me. I will close. But remain your loving Husband.

G.D. Vanderveer
Master U.S. Steam Transport Ironsides
Washington D.C.

P.S. I expect this will be some days reaching you.

Maps

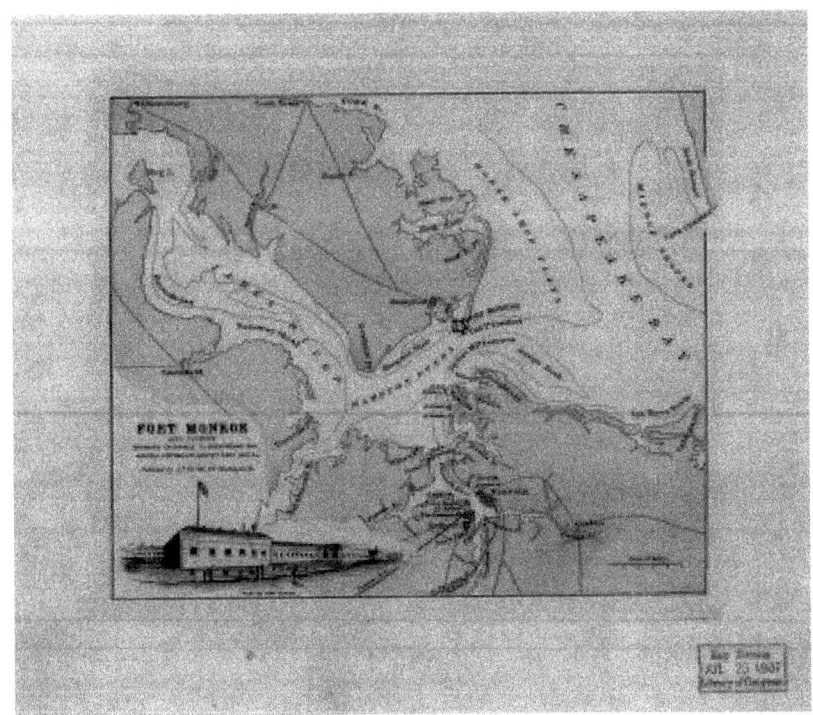

Fort Monroe

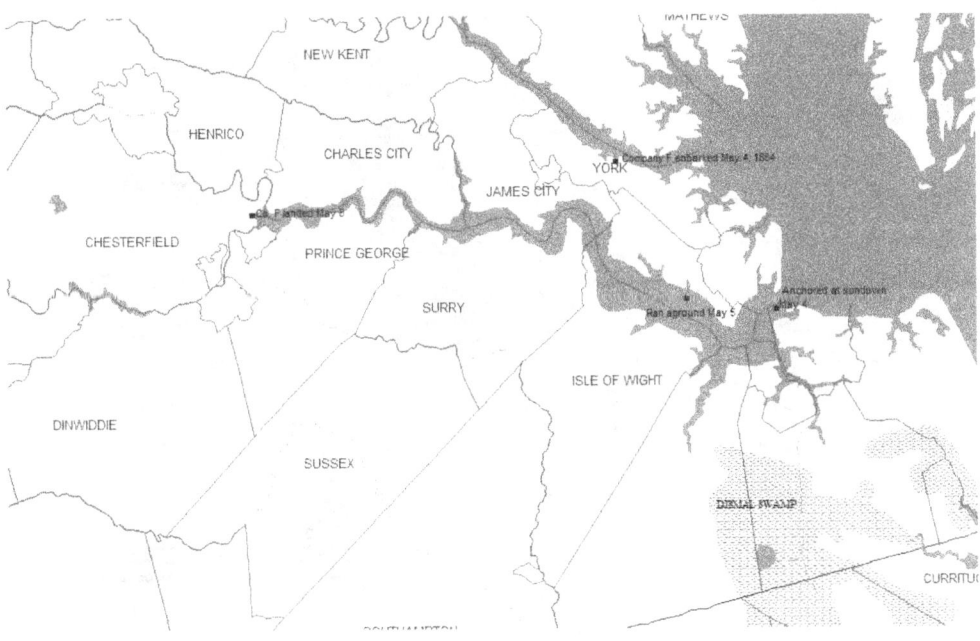

Locations of Company F from embarkation on May 4 through May 6, 1864

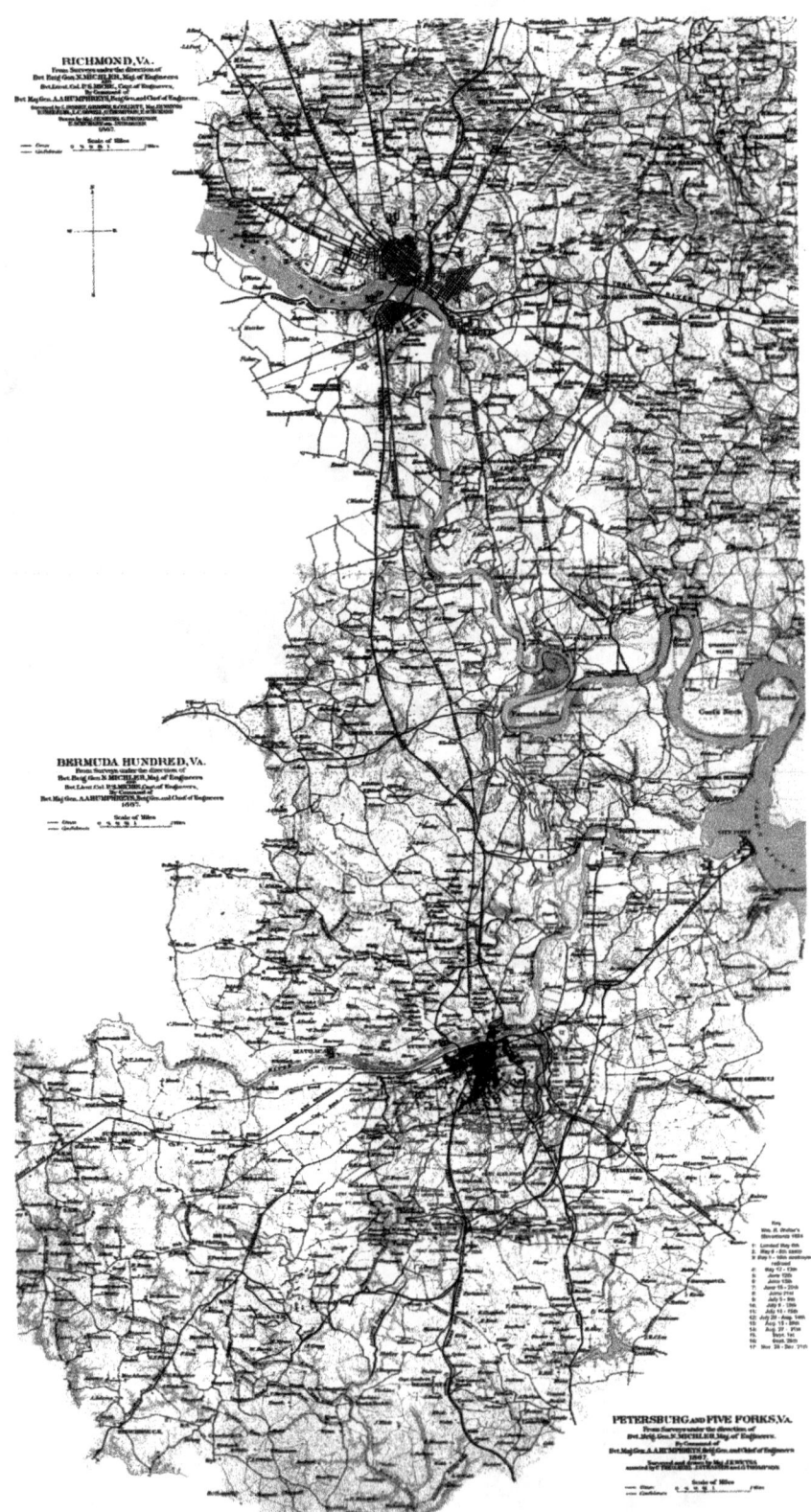

Locations of Company F, May 7 – December 31, 1864

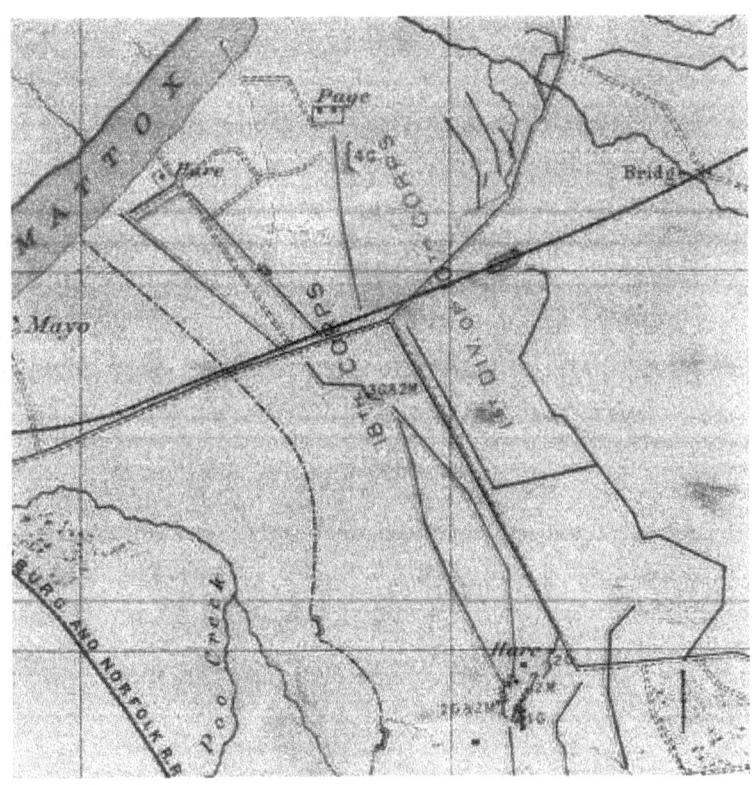
Location of the 18th Corps June 15 – August 26, 1864.

Close up of batteries June 15 – August 26, 1864.

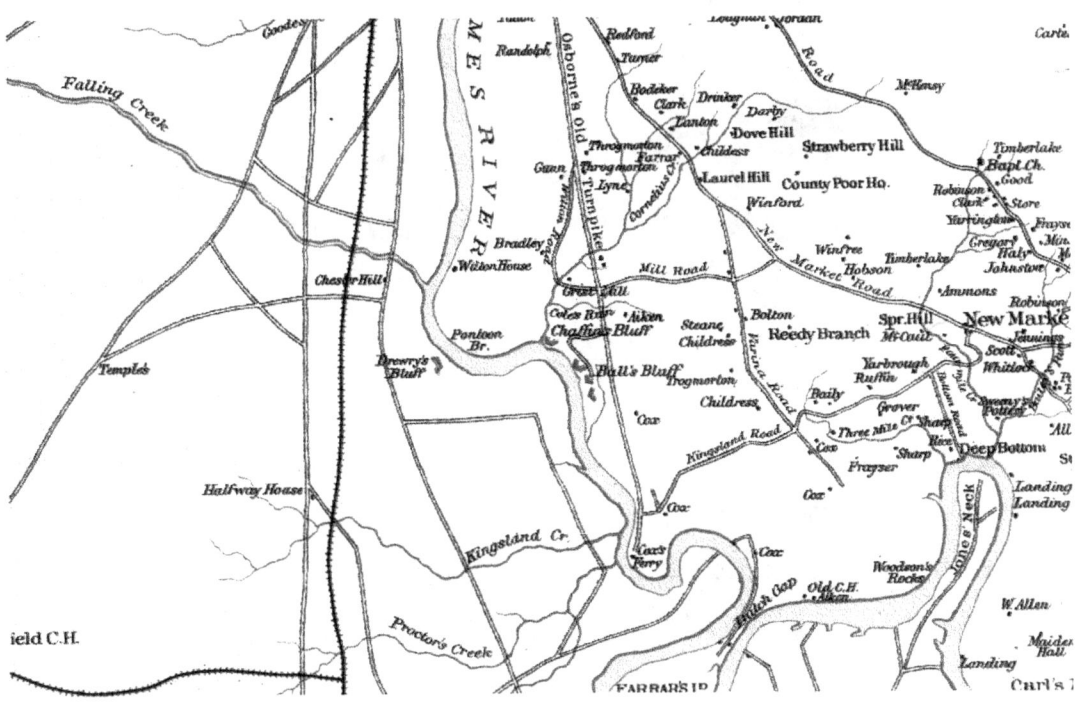

Drewry's Bluff to Deep Bottom including Chaffin's Farm 1864

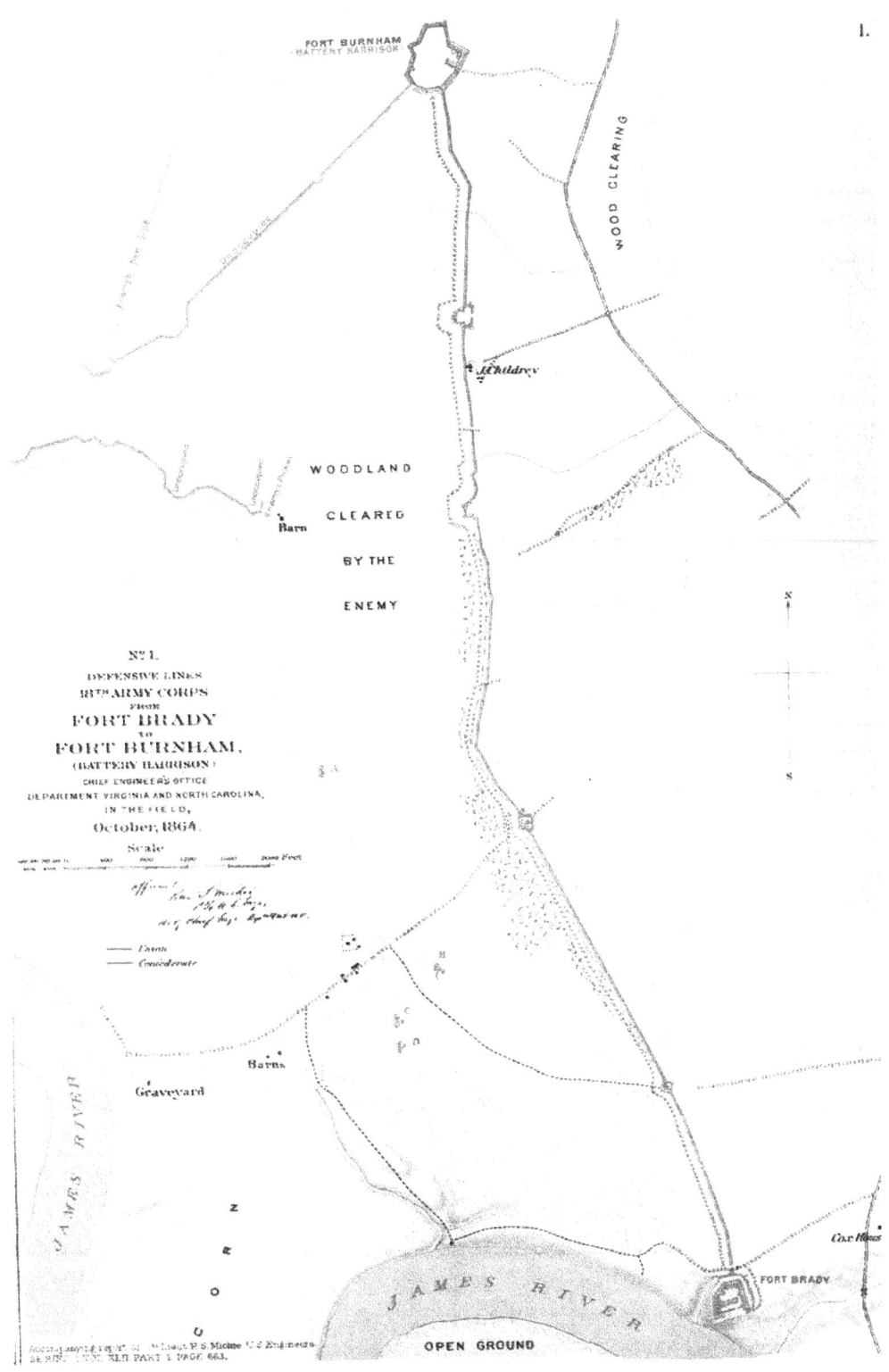

Diary entry December 4, 1864: Jesse White & Several others of the 97th Regiment came down to see Ed. We all went over to look at the captured Fort Harrison.

Photographs

188th Pennsylvania Volunteers Infantry Banner

The Lincoln Gun, Fortress Monroe, Virginia

Captain of the Port's office and Hygeia Dining Saloon
Fortress Monroe, Virginia

City Point, Virginia with boats on the James River

An unidentified fortification at Petersburg

Pontoon bridge across the Appomattox River

Soldiers await transportation to medical help

Hospital tents at City Point, Virginia

Three surgeons of the 9th Corps hospital
(*Perhaps one is Joseph Taylor?*)

Fort Burnham / Harrison

General Charles Jackson Paine

Chesapeake Hospital, Fortress Monroe, VA

Union 18th Corps badge

GAR members lapel pin

Bibliography

These are references from the *Army Military History Institute*: http://www.carlisle.army.mil/ahec/index.htm

- **Bates, Samuel P.**; History of the Pennsylvania Volunteers, 1861-5. Wilmington, NC: Broadfoot, 1993. Vol. 9, pp. 252-78 (14 photocopied pages). E527B32.1993v9. (Brief history and roster of the regiment).
- **Dyer, Frederick H. A**; Compendium of the War of the Rebellion. Vol. 2. Dayton, OH: Morningside, 1979. Ref. See p. 1623 (1 photocopied page) for a concise summary of the regiment's service.
- **Sauers, Richard A.**; Advance the Colors! Pennsylvania Civil War Battle Flags. Vol. 2. Hbg, PA: Capitol Preservation Comm, 1991. pp. 489-91 (3 photocopied pages). E527.4S38.1991v2. (Brief unit history with emphasis on the regimental flags).

Photo Records from the *Army Military History Institute*:

- The *Army Military History Institute* Photo Archive includes images of individuals of this unit. The following pertinent personal papers are in the Institute's Manuscript Archive: DeHaven, James M. - CWMiscColl (Enlisted man's letters, Jun 14, 1865) Richards, Jacob B. - CWMiscColl (Enlisted man's letters, Apr 30-Jun 27, 1864) Shinkle, Hiram R. - LeighColl, Bk 29: 46-47 (Officer's letters, May 25, 1864-Oct 30, 1865)

Title: <u>History of the Pennsylvania Volunteers</u>; Author: Samuel P. Bates. Includes: names of 188th enlisted and soldiers, time served, rank and Company

Title: <u>Advance the Colors</u>; Author: Richard A. Sauers. Contains: Photo of 188th Regimental Flag and history of bearer of colors. Vol. II. pages 489-491.

Title: Regimental Histories: Author: TBD Contains: 188th PA Vols regimental history on page 1623. Contains: 3rd Hvy Arty (152nd) regimental history on page. page 1571.

Title: <u>History of 188th Regiment Pennsylvania Volunteers</u>, Corn Exchange Regiment.... Phila: Smith, 1905. pp. 294-301. E527.5.118PA.P453. Execution of 5 deserters, Aug 1863.

Schmutz, George J. ; PAPERS, n.d. 2 vols. Papers consist of Schmutz's memoirs in two volumes on the history of the 188th Regiment Pennsylvania Infantry Volunteers. Gives a complete roster of the 188th and some of Schmutz's family history. Ms92-047.

Photos; The Civil War Home Page http://www.civil-war.net:
Three Surgeons of 1st Division, 9th Corps - Petersburg, VA, October 1864
Medical and Hospitals
http://www.civil-war.net/cw_images/files/images/291.jpg

583. Chesapeake Hospital and Grounds - Hampton, VA
Medical and Hospitals
http://www.civil-war.net/cw-images/files/images/583.jpg

561. View of Waterfront with Federal Supply Boats - City Point, VA
Navy Units and Ships
http://www.civil-war.net/cw_images/files/images/561.jpg

General Charles Jackson Paine
http://www.generalsandbrevets.com/ngp/painecj.htm

And all further battle scenes and forts: http://www.civil-war.net/cw-images/files/

Photos and obituary of William Harvey Walter: personal property of Carol-Lynn Sappé

Photo of Steamship Metamora; Detroit Publishing Co., publisher, Medium 1 negative : glass ; 8 x 10 in. Call Number LC-D4-9093 REPRODUCTION NUMBER LC-D4-9093 DLC (b&w glass neg.) Part of Detroit Publishing Company Photograph Collection Repository Library of Congress Prints and Photographs Division Washington, D.C. 20540 USA

Map of Fort Monroe; http://www.ushistoricalarchive.com/civilwar/va1/67.gif

Map of the country between Richmond and Petersburg; Negative 5605 Map PW 6149 Gilmer 1864 http://www.libs.uga.edu/darchive/hargrett/maps/civil.html

Map of Bermuda Hundred. From Surveys under the direction of Bvt. Brig. Gen. N. Michler, Maj. Of Engineers and Bvt. Lieut. Col. P.S. Michie, Capt. Of Engineers By Command of Bvt. Maj. Gen. A.A. Humphreys, Brig. Gen. & Chief of Engineers. 1867. U.S. War Department, Weyss, John E.; N.Y. Lithographing, Engraving & Printing Co.;

Map of Petersburg And Five Forks. From Surveys under the direction of Bvt. Brig. Gen. N. Michler, Maj. Of Engineers and Bvt. Lieut. Col. P.S. Michie, Capt. Of Engineers By Command of Bvt. Maj. Gen. A.A. Humphreys, Brig. Gen. & Chief of Engineers. 1867. U.S. War Department, Weyss, John E.; N.Y. Lithographing, Engraving & Printing Co.;

Glossary of Names

A

Abel, William D. — Company A, Private, mustered in February 6, 1864, killed at Drury's Bluff, VA, May 16, 1864.

Allen, Thomas — Company C, Private, mustered in October 28, 1682, discharged October 18, 1865 - experation of term.

Armstrong, Ben — Friend from Chester County, Pennsylvania. No further information has been found at this time.

Arnold, B. Z — Not a member of 188th PA Volunteers, no further information available; B.Z. Arnold, No. 1330 Lombard Street, Philadelphia.

Austin, John — Company F, First Lieutenant, mustered in March 23, 1863, dismissed Feb. 1, 1865

B

Ball, David W. W. — Company G, First Lieutenant, mustered in Dec. 19, 1863, mustered out with company Dec. 14, 1865, address upon mustering out: D.W.W. Ball, Ellsworth No. 1016, Philadelphia, Pa.

Baxter, Francis — Company F, Private, mustered in May 7, 1863, discharged by General Order, May 13, 1865

Beers, Lewis R. — Company F, Corporal, mustered in Jan. 26, 1863, wounded, with loss of leg, at Fort Harrison, Va., Sept. 29, 1864, discharged by General Order, Nov. 1865.

Benliss — Male nurse W. Mellan Hospital Fort Monroe; without a first name or rank at this time a closer identification in not possible.

Blain, George A. — Company F, Private, mustered in Jan. 5, 1863, deserted July 12, 1864

Blair, Andrew — Company A, Private, mustered in Jan. 2, 1864, mustered out with company Dec. 14, 1865

Bowen, S. J. — Sayles J. Bowen appointed City Post Master, Washington, D.C. March 16 1863

Breel, Harry E. — Company I, Captain, mustered in Feb. 13, 1863, died Sept. 22, of wounds received at Cold Harbor, Va., June 2, 1864.

Brooke, F.M. — Company I, Private, 29th Pennsylvania Military Infantry

Broomall, John Martin — 1816-1894, noted attorney, author, originator and director of the Delaware County Mutual
Insurance Company, state politician and president of the Delaware County Institute of Science. A renaissance man of his day he was well admired.

Brown, Alonzo — Company F, Private, mustered in Feb. 2, 1863, killed near Petersburg, Va., July 30, 1864

Brownlow, William Gannaway — An itinerant Methodist minister, was an intriguing political figure during the Civil War.
Parson Brownlow was pro-slavery but opposed to secession and wrote fiery articles for his "Brownlow's Knoxville Whig" which he founded in 1849. Arrested in 1861 by the Confederate authorities for his views, he was encouraged to leave the south and did so, traveling about the north giving speeches condemning the Confederacy. Born in Virginia, Brownlow had little formal education but went on to become Governor of Tennessee, 1865 – 1869 and then was elected to the U.S. Senate and served from 1869 – 1875.

Bryner, Samuel — Company F, Private, mustered in Feb. 24, 1864, mustered out with the company Dec. 14, 1865

Buckley, Curnell	Company F, Private, mustered in Jan. 11, 1864, mustered out with company Dec. 14, 1865
Burns, John W.	Company D, Sergeant, mustered in Feb. 23, 1864, mustered out with company Dec. 14, 1865

C

Carel, William	Company C, Private, mustered in Jan. 15, 1864, drowned at Broadway Landing, Va., May 21st, 1864, name also spelled Carroll.
Cassidy, Peter P.	Company K, Second Lieutenant, mustered in June 8, 1863, wounded at Cold Harbor, Va., June 5, 1864, discharged on Surgeon's certificate, Sept. 20, 1864.
Chamerlan, M.	Not a member of 188th PA Volunteers, no further information available; M. Chamerlan, No. 221 North 15th St., Philadelphia.
Chase, Theodore	Promoted to Captain of a Colored Regiment on May 11, 1864
Christy, Samuel H.	Company F, Private, mustered in Dec. 30, 1863, died at Hampton, Va., Nov. 24, 1864, of wounds received at Fort Harrison, Sept. 29, 1864.
Col. Henry	Colonel Henry L. Cake, 96th Regiment, Pennsylvania Infantry, on July 10th, the 96th was relieved from the Petersburg front and marched to City Point where it was transported to Washington D.C.
Collison, Theodore	Company F, Private, mustered in Jan. 18, 1864, mustered out with company Dec. 14, 1865, name also spelled Cullison.
Corp. Gamble	See Gamble, Peter
Costello, Bartley	Company I, Corporal, 2nd Pennsylvania Heavy Artillery
Crahan, Martin	Company F, Sergeant, mustered in Nov. 5, 1862, discharged by General Order, Sept. 9, 1865, name also spelled Crayon, Creahan, Croagham.
Cyrus Donty	Company F, Private, mustered in Feb. 11, 1864, wounded, with loss of arm at Fort Harrison, Va., Sept. 29, 1864, discharge by General order, July 13, 1865, name also spelled Doubty or Dowty

D

Davis, Byron F.	Company F, mustered in Jan. 19, 1863, transferred to Company C as Sergeant Major, promoted from 1st Lieutenant of that company to Adjutant and reassigned to regiment, mustered out with regiment Dec. 14, 1865.
Dedin, Arizalla S.	Born 1841, father was a shoemaker in East Brandywine, Pa., known as Kate.
Dial, Abraham S.	Company F & E, Captain, Aug. 25, 1863, mustered out with company Dec. 14, 1855, also known by the name Absolom S. Dial, known address upon mustering out: Mr. A.S. Dial, Pemyopolis, Fayette Co, Pa/
Dickerson, Allison I.	Company F, Private, mustered in Feb. 19, 1864, discharged on Surgeon's certificate, Oct. 25, 1864
Dickson, Henry B.	Company F, Captain, mustered in Sept. 15, 1862, killed at Chaffin's Farm, Va., Sept. 30, 1864
Dixon, Maris	Friend from Kennett, Chester County, PA, brother of James Dixon.

E

Eachus, Ammon	Friend from Chester County, Pennsylvania. Many Eachus families lived in Chester and Delaware counties at the time. Several list Ammon as a son. At this time a closer identification in not possible.

Elwood, Mary E.	Born 1847 in Ireland and resided with her uncle Hugh Sterling in Brandywine Hundred, Delaware in 1860. She is a known friend but how she and William met can only be conjectured.
Etter, David C.	Company G, Corporal, mustered in Dec. 21, 1863, mustered out with company, Dec. 14, 1865.
Evans, Samuel D.	Company F, Private, mustered in June 22, 1863, deserted Aug. 12, 1865.

F

Farnsworth, Henry T.	Company D, Private, mustered in Sept. 24, 1863, discharged by General Order June 18, 1865.

G

Garrit, George W.	Company E, Sergeant, mustered in February 25, 1864, promoted to Corporal, August 27, 1864 – to Sergeant, April 18, 1865, mustered out with company December 14, 1865.
Gamble, Peter	Company E, Sergeant, 3rd Heavy Artillery Regiment Pennsylvania on 21 Nov 1863. Promoted to Full Sergeant on 25 Mar 1864, mustered out with company, November 9, 1865 at Fort Monroe, VA. Last known address at end of war: Peter Gamble, Manchester, Ocean Co., NJ.
Geiser, Anthony	Company F, Corporal, mustered in Dec. 22, 1863, captured (no place given), mustered out with company December 14, 1865.
Gilbert, Elwood	203rd Pennsylvania Volunteers, no other information available.
Gregg, John G.	Company D, Lieutenant Colonel, mustered in Sept. 16, 1862, wounded at Cold Harbor, Va., June 1, 1864, career soldier.

H

Hale, William Harry	Company F, latter assigned to Company H, Private, mustered in Feb. 4, 1864, deserted Sept. 5,1865.
Hamilton, George	Company F, Private, mustered in April 22, 1863, absent, in arrest, at muster out.
Harvey, Ann J.	Born 1837, Philadelphia, Pa., daughter of James Harvey.
Harvey, Jacob	Born 1827, a school teacher in Fairville, Pa., a farm village on the border with Delaware. He was married to Margaret and had two sons, Pusey and Harry. Later Chester county superintendent of schools.
Haslehurst	Does not appear among the ranks of the 188th Penna. Vols. He may have been assigned to another regiment.
Hicks, Alfred J.	Company F, 183rd Pennsylvania Volunteers, Private, mustered in Feb. 8, 1864, mustered out with company, July 13, 1865.
Hoffner, William	Company C, Private, mustered in Feb. 15, 1864, mustered out with company, Dec. 14, 1865.
Hollingsworth, Mary E. (Emma)	Born 1841 at Kennett Square, Pennsylvania, daughter of Caleb Hollingsworth and Mary H. Kirk, married Caleb Wright. William Harvey Walter's 2nd cousin through his stepmother Elizabeth Jane Dutton.
Horn, William C.	Company A, mustered in March 17, 1864, listed as deserted however, the date of his desertion and date of soldier falling over board correspond.
Howell, E.	At this time not enough information to determine who this is or where he/she is from.
Hysleman, Peter T.	208th Regular Pennsylvania Infantry, Private.

J

James, Leon — Storeowner in Upper Providence, Pennsylvania.

Jeffers, James H. — Company F, entered as Sergeant but demoted to Private, mustered in Feb. 11, 1862, died at
Philadelphia, Pa., Feb. 15, 1865.

Johnson, Isaac — A family friend. From 1874 – 1884, he was Recorder of Deeds for Delaware County, Pa., in 1877 he   was director of the Grammar School located at Media, Pa., and in Dec. of 1883 he was admitted to the Bar in the county.

Joyce, Michael J. — Company F, Sergeant Major, mustered in June 2, 1863, not on mustered out roles.

Joyce, Michael J. — Company F, Sergeant Major, mustered in June 27, 1863, mustered out with regimen, Dec. 14, 1865.

K

Kern, Francis I. — Company F & S, Surgeon, mustered in Aug. 22, 1863, discharged on Surgeon's certificate, July 9, 1864.

Kirk, Rosanna — Born 1842 in Upper Providence, Pa. Father John Kirk was a farmer. "Rosie" was to become Mrs.
William Harvey Walter.

L

Long, Ben — A common name in Pennsylvania and Delaware. At this time no further information available.

Longaker, B. — Benjamin B. Longaker, born 1848, son of Joseph Longaker, master miller of Radnor, Pennsylvania.

Lush, Theodore — Company F, Private, mustered in Nov. 7, 1861, mustered out with company, Dec. 14, 1865.

M

McCluen, Edward L. — Company F, First Lieutenant, mustered in Dec. 23, 1863, mustered out with company Dec. 14, 1865.

McElrath, John — Company B, Sergeant, mustered in March 23, 1863, died at Hampton, Va., Oct. 9, 1864 of wounds received at Fort Harrison, Va., Sept. 29, 1864, also known as McIlrath.

McLaughlin, John A.M. — Company F, Private, mustered in Jan. 1, 1864, mustered out with the company Dec. 14, 1865,
name also spelled McGlaughlin.

McMichael, Albert — Company F, Private, mustered in Jan. 27, 1863, mustered out with company Dec. 14, 1865

McNeil, George — Company F, First Lieutenant, name also spelled McNeal or McNiel, mustered in Oct. 28, 1863, died at Fortress Monroe, Oct. 14, 1864, of wounds received at Fort Harrison, Sept. 29, 1864.

Milles, Charles — From Radnor, PA in 1864, he was born in Ireland, 1836, worked as a farm hand then as a carpenter.

Moore, Carle H. — Company H, Private, mustered in March 26, 1864, mustered out with company, Dec. 14, 1865.

Moore, William — Company F, Sergeant, mustered in Feb. 9, 1864, mustered out with company Dec. 14, 1865.

Myers, David S. — Company I, Sergeant, mustered in Oct. 20, 1862, discharged Oct. 24, 1865, expiration of term.

N

Naomi — Most likely this is Naomi Sharpless, a cousin.

Noll, Jacob — Company B, transferred to Company F, Sept. 29, 1863, Private, mustered in Feb. 10, 1863, captured – absent, at Camp Parole, Annapolis, Md., at muster out.

Normall, Edwin — Friend from Delaware County, Pa. however no further information can be determined at this time.

O

O'Brian, John — Company F, Private, mustered in March 12, 1864, wounded at Fort Harrison, Va., Sept. 29, 1864, discharged by General Order, June 28, 1865.

P

Paine, Charles Jackson — General, commanded 1st then 3rd Divn/XXV Corps at Petersburg, distinguished himself in the Civil War by leading colored troops.

Palmer, John E. — Company F, Private, mustered in June 22, 1863, mustered out with company Dec. 14, 1865

Palmer, John H. — Company F, Private, mustered in Jan. 27, 1863, mustered out with company Dec. 14, 1865.

Paullin, Benjamin F. — Company D, Sergeant, mustered in November 20, 1862, promoted to Sergeant May 1, 1864 – discharged November 21, 1865 – expiration of term: B.F. Paulding, Wood Street Above 16th, Philadelphia.

Petterson — Thomas F. Peterson, Company I, 183rd Pennsylvania Volunteers, mustered in March 8, 1864, deserted then returned, mustered out with the company July 13, 1865.

Phillips, Will — William G., born 1820, a spoke and wagon builder in Mill Creek Hundred, Delaware, married to Hannah I.

Pitt, Joseph — Company F, Corporal, mustered in April 1, 1864, deserted April 27, 1864.

Poole, Joe — Joseph, born 1830 in Pennsylvania, owned farm in Mill Creek Hundred, Delaware, married to Sarah, daughter: Mary Ann Poole.

Poole, Thomas — Son of J. Morten Poole, Master Merchant of Ward I, Wilmington, Delaware.

Potter, Joseph K. — Company F, Corporal, mustered in Nov. 11, 1863, accidentally killed on South Side Rail Road, Petersburg, Va., Dec. 1, 1864.

R

Reen, Frederick A. — Company F transferred to Company B, Major, mustered in Feb. 20, 1864, promoted from Private to 2nd Lt. March 31, 1864, to 1st Lt. July 22, 1864, to Capt. Dec. 14, 1864, to Maj. Nov. 26, 1865, wounded at Fort Harrison, Va., Sept. 29, 1864, mustered out with company, Dec. 14, 1865, known address upon mustering out: Fred A Reen, Liverpool Rd, Perry Co, Pa.

Reinboth, Henry B. — Company F, Captain, mustered in Nov. 22, 1862, discharged by special order May 17, 1865.

Rood, Calvin S. — Company A, Corporal and Musician, mustered in April 1, 1864, mustered out with company, Dec. 14, 1865, also known by Alvin S. Road.

Roberts, Benjamin — Company A, reduced to rank of Private.

Robertson, Anthony — Was assigned to Company F, Private, mustered in Dec. 12, 1863, wounded at Fort Harrison, Va., Sept. 29, 1864, discharged on Surgeons Certificate, Nov. 9, 1864.

Rush, John — Company H, Private, mustered in Feb. 1, 1864, mustered out with company Dec. 14, 1865.

Ryan, John — Company F, Private, mustered in Sept. 20, 1862, promoted to 2nd. Lt., 118th Regiment, U.S.C.T., Dec. 7, 1864, died at Brownsville, Texas, Oct. 2, 1865, of wounds received in action.

S

Sands, George — Company F, Private, mustered in Nov. 21, 1862, discharged Nov. 21, 1865, expiration of term.

Sergeant Godfrey — 42nd Pennsylvania Volunteers and 1st Pennsylvania Rifles, Company A.

Sharpless, John — Son of Caleb, farmer, and Elizabeth Sharpless of Christiana Hundred, Delaware.

Sharpless, Joshua K.	Brother of Phebe Anna Sharpless, born 1835, son of Jacob W. Sharpless, born 1806, he was a master stone mason in Pennsbury, Pa.
Sharpless, Phebe Anna	Born 1843 in Pennsbury Township, Pennsylvania, daughter of Jacob N. Sharpless, remained a spinster later living with her brother Joshua K. Sharpless in Wilmington, Delaware.
Shinkle, Hiram R.	Company E, Captain, mustered in March 3, 1863, killed while attacking Fort Darling at Drewry's Bluff, Va., May 16th, 1864.
Shorburn	Without a first name or rank a closer identification in not possible at this time.
Singles, William H.	Company F, Private, mustered in Feb. 24, 1864, discharged by General Order, May 26, 1865.
Smith, James	Company F, Private, mustered in July 21, 1863, mustered out with the company Dec. 14, 1865.
Smith, Jarvis	Research shows 8 Jarvis Smith's served during the Civil War but none from Maine; the only listing in the diary is his address, Jarvis Smith, Holton Co., Maine.
Spengler, Theodore	Company F & S, Regimental Quarter Master, 188th Pennsylvania Volunteers.
Spout, George	Company F, Private, mustered in Feb. 20, 1864, died near Petersburg, Va., Aug. 16, 1864, also listed as Sprout.
Sterner, Ross R.	Company F, Sergeant, mustered in Nov. 12, 1861, mustered out with company, Dec. 14, 1865. known address upon mustering out: Ross R. Sterner, Addison, Somerset Co, Penna.
Stewart, Frank	203rd Pennsylvania Volunteers.
Sutler	A person who followed an army or maintained a store on an army post to sell provisions to the soldiers.

T

Taylor, Joseph	9th Corps. Brigade Surgeon.
Terest	Without a first name or rank a closer identification in not possible at this time.
Thomas, Evan	Company B 203rd Pennsylvania Infantry, enlisted as a Private on August 29, 1864, was absent at hospital when unit mustered out June 22, 1865.
Thomas, W. B.	Born 1812, head clerk at the Philadelphia Custom House, resided in Ward 17 at 2nd and Enum Str. In 1870.

V

Vanleer, George A.	Company F, Private, mustered in Jan. 30, 1864, deserted Sept. 1865, also known as George W. Vanleer.
Velotte, Felix	A well to do farmer and land owner of Marple, Delaware County, Pennsylvania. He was born in France and was the father of Joseph D., Mary and Penrose Vellote.
Velotte, Joseph D.	Born 1837, brother of Mary Velotte and friend to William and Townsend. Joseph owned the Rose Tree Hotel in Upper Providence township in 1868.
Velotte, Mary	Born 1839, daughter of Felix and Abigail Velotte of Marple, Delaware County, Pa. The Walter and Velotte families were close friends.
Velotte, Penrose	Born 1845, brother of Joseph D. and Mary Velotte, son of Felix Velotte.

W

Washburn, Wesley	As of this date has not been identified however, this watch is still in the family.
Welsh, Edward	Company F, Private, mustered in Dec. 29, 1863, discharged on Surgeon's certificate, Aug. 25, 1865, name also listed as Walch and Welch.

Wetzler	Without a first name or rank a closer identification in not possible at this time.
White, Jesse	Company F, 97th Pennsylvania Infantry, rank in: Private, rank out: Musician, prior to enlisting boarded in Ward 13, Philadelphia, Pennsylvania.
White, William	Born 1841 in Delaware, was apprenticed to Nathan Edwards of Pocopson, Pa. as a carpenter. A friend of William and Townsend.
Willard	Without a first name or rank a closer identification in not possible at this time.
Williams, Harry	Company F, Corporal, mustered in Jan. 30, 1864, mustered out with company Dec. 14, 1865, his address after mustering out: H. Williams, No. 27 Haighurst Avenue, Slead, N.J.
Williamson, Louis	Company F, Sergeant, mustered in Dec. 18, 1863, mustered out with company Dec. 14, 1865
Worrell, Ellwood M.	Media Mill owner. Born July 30, 1842, Upper Providence, Delaware County, Pennsylvania; died September 13, 1913, Strodia Mill, Pennsylvania. Son of Joseph Worrell and Catherine Palmer.

Footnotes

[1] Nield's Independent Battery, Delaware Light Artillery

Organized at Wilmington, Del., August 30, 1862. Ordered to Washington, D. C., September 1862. Attached to Camp Barry, Defenses of Washington, D. C., to February 1863. Camp Barry, Defenses of Washington, 22nd Army Corps, to April 1863. Unattached Artillery, 7th Army Corps, Dept. of Virginia, to June 1863. Artillery, 1st Division, 7th Army Corps, to July 1863. Camp Barry, 22nd Army Corps, to August 1863. Dept. of the East to October 1863. Camp Barry, 22nd Army Corps, to February 1864. Defenses of New Orleans, La., Dept. of the Gulf, to July 1864. Artillery, 1st Division, 19th Army Corps, Dept. of the Gulf, to August 1864. Artillery, 3rd Division, 19th Army Corps, Dept. of the Gulf, to November 1864. Unassigned Artillery, Reserve Corps, Military Division West Mississippi, to December 1864. Artillery, 2nd Division, 7th Army Corps, Dept. of Arkansas, to June 1865.

SERVICE. -Duty in the Defenses of Washington, D.C., till April 1863. Ordered to Norfolk, Va., April 18. Siege of Norfolk April 21-May 4. Dix's Peninsula Campaign June 23-July 8. Ordered to Washington, D. C., July 8, and duty in the defenses of that city till August. At New York City, Dept. of the East, till September 12, and at Light Artillery Camp of Instruction, Defenses of Washington, till February 1864. Ordered to Dept. of the Gulf, and at New Orleans, La., till March 2. Ordered to Franklin March 2. Red River Campaign March 10-May 22. Advance from Franklin to Alexandria, La., March 15-26. Battles of Sabine Cross Roads April 8 and Pleasant Hill April 9 (Reserve). At Grand Ecore April 10-22. Cane River Crossing April 23. At Alexandria April 26-May 13. Retreat to Morganza May 13-20. At Morganza till October 16. Ordered to mouth of White River and duty there and at Morganza till December. Ordered to Arkansas December 11. Duty at mouth of White River and at Little Rock, Ark., till June 1865. Mustered out June 23, and discharged from service July 5, 1865.

Battery lost 6 by disease during service. NARA http://www.archives.gov/research_room

[2] The story of Delaware County during the long years of the Civil War is almost a counterpart of every locality of the like character in the Northern States. The enormous drain upon the resources of the nation, the wholesale destruction of life and property stimulated an unusual activity in business to keep pace with the demand, and employed the surplus labor at high wages. The various industrial establishments ran day and night, and yet the market was often unable to furnish goods as rapidly as they were required. As the war advanced the Union armies were necessarily compelled to increase their numbers; every city, town or State, which was won by Northern troops required to be held by the bayonet, while long lines of communication, lengthening as the armies advanced, must be maintained uninterrupted. Hence it became absolutely essential that a great number of men should be called to the field and as recruiting began to flag, the government was compelled to provide by law for compulsory military service. To that end, in the early summer of 1862, the President notified the various States that unless the required troops were furnished he would call for a conscription in accordance with the act of Congress. In Delaware County, as throughout the North, there was a popular feeling against the measure, and it was determined, if possible, to avoid the enforcement of the law, by offering bounties to men to enlist.

Taken from Henry Graham Ashmead's History of Delaware County, Philadelphia; L.H. Everts & Co., 1884

[3] Fortress Monroe, located at the confluence of the James River and Chesapeake Bay. Connected by a land bridge to Hampton, Va. The present fort was built between 1819 and 1834 but there had been previous military installations since 1609. At that time the English settlers called the area Point Comfort and the first fort was named Fort Algernourne. Several others followed but these forts were short lived. During the War of 1812 the United States realized it needed to improve protection for its ports and cities and so Fort Monroe was the first of these new defenses to be built. Thanks to its location this Union fort was able to repel Confederate attacks and to extend Union control along the coasts as far south as South Carolina. Land assaults were also launched from the fort. The battle of Big Bethel in June 1861, Major General George McClellan's Peninsula Campaign of 1862 and the siege of Suffolk in 1863. In 1864 the Army of the James was formed at Fort Monroe. Fort Monroe is also the place at which Major General Benjamin Butler made his famous "contraband" decision, by which escaping slaves reaching Union lines would not be returned to bondage. Former Confederate President, Jefferson Davis, was a prisoner here for two years.

[4] There is no record of William having a brother Joe. He is mentioned later in the diary by the same reference. William is referring to his friend Joseph D. Velotte.

[5] William Gannaway Brownlow, an itinerant Methodist minister, was an intriguing political figure during the Civil War. Parson Brownlow was pro-slavery but opposed to secession and wrote fiery articles for his "Brownlow's Knoxville Whig" which he founded in 1849. Arrested in 1861 by the Confederate authorities for his views, he was encouraged to leave the south and did so, traveling about the north giving speeches condemning the Confederacy. Born in Virginia, Brownlow had little formal education but went on to become Governor of Tennessee, 1865 – 1869 and then was elected to the U.S. Senate and served from 1869 – 1875.

[6] Matthew Hospital was more then likely attached to Fortress Monroe. The only hospital found listed for Hampton, Va. is Chesapeake Hospital. See footnote #73

[7] On March 1, 1855, Dr. D.A. Vernon & Thomas V. Cooper printed the first issue of the *Media Advertiser* in Media, PA. This newspaper changed its name to the *Media Advertiser and Delaware County American* on February 27, 1856 and then on March 2, 1859 became known as the *Delaware County American*.

[8] "Old" Company F, 188th Pennsylvania Volunteers

[9] O'Niel Oak Bridge, one of the bridges connecting Fortress Monroe to Hampton, Va.

[10] Delaware County Bounty; see footnote #2

[11] A prison camp for Confederate prisoners of war built at Point Lookout, Md. It was located at the tip of the peninsula where the Potomac River enters Chesapeake Bay. The prison camp was in operation from August, 1863 until June, 1865.

[12] The new company formed: Company F of the 188th Pennsylvania Volunteers.

[13] George McNeil; Company F, First Lieutenant, name also spelled McNeal or McNiel, mustered in Oct. 28, 1863, died at Fortress Monroe, Oct. 14, 1864, of wounds received at Fort Harrison, Sept. 29, 1864

[14] Camp Hamilton was located about one mile from Fortress Monroe in Hampton, Va.

[15] Soldiers Burying Ground, the main cemetery at Fortress Monroe, Va.

[16] Colored Troops at the time of the Civil War were made up of run away slaves and free Blacks from the Northern States. Approximately 94'000 were ex-slaves from the Confederacy, 44'000 were ex-slaves or freemen from the boarder states and the rest recruited from the northern states and Colorado territory. Approximately 164 regiments, 10 batteries of light artillery, independent units, Pioneer Corps, and unassigned USCT units were organized in the Confederate States by the Union Army or as state militia in the North. They were redesignated as United States Colored Troops after the establishment of the Bureau of Colored Troops on May 22, 1863. http://www.coax.net/people/lwf/usct.htm

[17] Yorktown, Va.; located at the confluence of the York and Chesapeake Bay, approximately 15 miles from Fortress Monroe, was an embarkation point and encampment for Union troops. Battle for Yorktown, April 16 – May 4, 1862; Marching from Fort Monroe, Major General George B. McClellan's army encountered Major General John B. Magruder's small Confederate army at Yorktown behind the Warwick River. http://americancivilwar.com/statepic/va/

[18] Henry B. Dickson; Company F, Captain, mustered in Sept. 15, 1862, killed at Chaffin's Farm, Va., Sept. 30, 1864

[19] William C. Horn; Company A, mustered in March 17, 1864, listed as deserted however, the date of his desertion and date of soldier falling over board correspond.

[20] City Point, main staging area for the siege of Petersburg and Richmond. Grant's headquarters, located at Appomattox Manor, at the confluence of the Appomattox and James River. Site of major Quarter Master depot and military hospital. Bermuda Hundred lay on the north side of the Appomattox River while City Point occupied the south bank.

[21] Steamboat News of Jersey, one of the numerous steamboats pressed into service by the War Department. According to the National Archives, Washington, DC, a "Record of Vessels Bought or Sold to the Federal Government, 1815 – 1923", the Quartermaster Department, War Department, purchased numerous sea worthy crafts, renamed them and put them to use in the war effort. Many of these same crafts were sold back to their original owners at the end of the conflict. Records of my family show that one such boat was the "Ironsides", owned by the Philadelphia Steam Propeller Company, Master G.D. Vanderveer, my Great Grandfather on my father's side of the family. This vessel was sold on April 16, 1862, renamed the Susan and saw service on the Chesapeake Bay and James River. It was resold to Master G.D. Vanderveer on March 21, 1866 at Philadelphia.

[22] Fort Darling was an earthen fort on the west bank of the James River, about five miles north of Bermuda Hundred. A line of trenches extended from this fort in a southwesterly direction to Proctor's Creek bridge on the Richmond & Petersburg Rail Road. On May 12th, Maj. Gen. Benjamin Butler moved his troops north and attached the Confederate line at Drewy's Bluff. This became known as the Proctor's Creek battle. It also goes by Drewy's Bluff or Fort Darling Battle. A Confederate victory as the Union troops fell back.

[23] Hiram R. Shinkle; Company E, Captain, mustered in March 3, 1863, killed while attacking Fort Darling at Drewry's Bluff, Va., May 16th, 1864

[24] Opium pills, the medicine of choice during the Civil War. Unfortunately it was also the start of many addictions for those for whom it was prescribed.

[25] William Carel; Company C, Private, mustered in Jan. 15, 1864, drowned at Broadway Landing, Va., May 21st, 1864, name also spelled Carroll.

[26] Metamora Steamship Built by Thomas Collyer in 1850 at his shipyard at the foot of East 21st Street, New York, New York.

[27] Mail Boat "J.Tucker; by 1820 more then 200 steamboats plied rivers and lakes. The Post Office department issued contracts to these vessels to carry mail.

[28] Curnell Buckley; Company F, Private, mustered in Jan. 11, 1864, mustered out with company Dec. 14, 1865

[29] West Point, a bend on the James River above Jamestown Island

[30] Chesapeake Hospital was located at Hampton, VA. and served as a medical facility for officers. Non-commissioned officers and enlisted men were taken to Hampton Hospital. Prior to the war the building served as a school for girls. Five surgeons were assigned to Chesapeake Hospital and it could accommodate 500 patients.

Hampton, Virginia. Chesapeake Hospital and grounds, December, 1864 from the Brady Civil War Photograph Collection (Library of Congress). LC-B811-840

[31] Fort Clifton was a Confederate fort located on a bluff at the junction of Swift Creek and the Appomattox River. From its position is controlled navigation on the river north of Petersburg. Built during the winter of 1863/64, the fort was never taken until the fall of Petersburg. The largest attack on this fort took place May 9th, 1864 when gun boats and units of the Union X and XVIII Corps attacked. This became known as the Swift Creek Battle.

[32] Francis I. Kern; Company F&S, Surgeon, mustered in Aug. 22, 1863, discharged on Surgeon's certificate, July 9, 1864

[33] The official record of enlistment as kept on file by the state or local government where the soldier enlisted. Used as proof to obtain payment and bounties promised.

[34] Great Fire in Petersburg; during heavy bombarding buildings within Petersburg caught fire. They were allowed to burn as most Confederate forces were occupied at the 1st Battle of Deep Bottom.

[35] On July 30th, 1864, the Union forces under the command of Maj. Gen. Ambrose E. Burnside, detonated a mine beneath Pegram's Salient thus blowing a gap in the Confederate line. Union forces began flowing through the gap but due to ineptness the Confederate forces under the command of Maj. Gen. William Mahon were able to seal the gap and turn the battle into a Confederate victory. Maj. Gen. Ambrose E. Burnside was relieved of duty for his role in this defeat.

[36] Village Record; The Village Record and Register and Examiner, began publication 1854 by John S. Bowen and James M. Meredith, originally named The Chester and Delaware Federalist, Dennis Whelen publisher, began publication in 1809.

[37] 18th Corp Hospital at Point of Rocks; across the pontoon bridge on the north side of the Appomatox River. Sunken Island and Cobbs Island can be seen from this point.

[38] Wiskey Punch was the remedy of the day for fever and ague. Made of whiskey, water and sugar, it may have also contain cloves and/or lemon if available.

[39] J.A.M. McLaughlin; Identified as John McLaughlin the day after he died, this John McLaughlin is not a member of the 188th Pennsylvania Volunteers. There are 147 John McLaughlin listed as Union soldiers. Research as to company and regiment continues.

[40] George Leary Steamboat; see footnote #21

[41] W. Mellan Hospital; located at Fortress Monroe, this hospital was for non-commissioned officers and enlisted men.

[42] Although William refers to this as Deep Bottom, the wounded were coming in from the fight at Fort Harrison which was taken. [On the night of the 28th, the entire corps was relieved, and moving silently, crossed the James on a muffled pontoon bridge, at Aiken's Landing, and just at day-break, commenced a cautious advance upon the enemy. His pickets were soon encountered and driven, and pushing on at quick time, through a thick wood with tangled undergrowth, the troops at length emerged upon open ground in front of, the rebel works, but a few hundred yards away. Fort Harrison, strongly built and bristling with cannon, was in their immediate front, and before the garrison was hardly aroused, the order to charge at double-quick was given. A long stretch of open ground was passed at a run, and though the enemy brought all his guns and his small arms to bear, he failed to get the range of the advancing troops, firing for the most part too high. At a point within fifty yards of the fort was a slight ravine, which stretched along in its front, capable of affording some protection, and here the line was re-formed, and the men took breath. They were now under a desperate fire, and to go forward was sure to entail heavy slaughter; but pausing only for a moment, the word was again given to charge; and without flinching, as one man the line sprang forward. A terrible volley. swept it, and many brave men fell. For an instant it seemed to waver; but only for an instant, and recovering, it dashed on, and the works were, carried. Fortunately, the men of the One Hundred and Eighty-eighth were' well schooled in the use of the Fortress guns, and instantly turned the guns of the fort upon the foe. The victory was complete. The rebel stronghold with all its guns, small arms, and many prisoners, was taken. General Ord; in command of the corps, and General Stannard, in command of the division;, were wounded, and General Burnham was killed. The First Division was soon rallied, and advanced upon Fort Gilmer, to the left, under cover of rebel gunboats on the James, and batteries posted along its banks; but it was repulsed, and suffered grievous slaughter in returning to the fort, Lieutenant George M'Neil receiving a mortal wound when close upon the rebel works. At nightfall, the troops were put to work in preparing the fort for effective defense and at dawn it had been reversed and presented a new face.] History of the Pennsylvania Volunteers, Samuel P. Bates

[43] Hospital Steamer Matilda; see footnote #21

[44] York Harbor; Yorktown Harbor, VA

[45] Michael J. Joyce; Company F, Sergeant Major, mustered in June 27, 1863, mustered out with regimen, Dec. 14, 1865

[46] Wesley Washburn to this date has not been identified however, this watch is still in the family.

[47] Steamboat Adelaide; see footnote #21

[48] Jacob Harvey, born 1827, was a school teacher in Fairville, Pa., a farm village on the border with Delaware. He was married to Margaret and had two sons, Pusey and Harry.

[49] Leon James Store, located in Upper Providence, Pennsylvania

[50] Joe, alias Bro. Joe refers to Joseph D. Velotte.

[51] Steamer Susan; see footnote #21

[52] Chaffin's Farm; a large open bluff on the James River north of City Point, was named for a local resident. The Battle of Chaffin's Farm, also known as New Market Heights and Fort Harrison, was fought September 29–September 30, 1864, as part of the Siege of Petersburg and the area afterwards used as a Union army staging point for attacks against Richmond.

[53] S.J. Bowen, appointed City Post Master, Washington, D.C. March 16 1863

[54] General Pain's Headquarters; this refers to Brevet Major General Charles Jackson Paine

[55] Fort Harrison was the strongest point on the line of defenses protecting the approaches to Richmond. From the fort you could see all the way to the James River. However, its garrison consisted of only 200 men and the guns so poor they were the scorn of the Confederate army. The Union forces were able to take the fort quickly and with minimum casualties. The Union forces quickly renamed the edifice Fort Burnham in honor of Gen. Burnham who fell during the attack.

[56] Theodore Chase, promoted to Captain of a Colored Regiment on May 11, 1864

[57] Theodore Lush; Company F, Private, mustered in Nov. 7, 1861, mustered out with company, Dec. 14, 1865

[58] John Martin Broomall, 1816-1894, noted attorney, author, originator and director of the Delaware County Mutual Insurance Company, state politician and president of the Delaware County Institute of Science. A renaissance man of his day he was well admired.

[59] W.B. Thomas; head clerk at the Philadelphia Custom House which at that time was located at 420 Chestnut Street. The building was used as a custom house from 1844 – 1932.

[60] Media Mills, one of the many mills that operated in and around Media, Pa. at that time. See Glossary of names: Ellwood M. Worrell

[61] Libby Prison; a Confederate prison located at Richmond, VA, it was infamous for its harsh conditions. The prison was housed in a three-story brick warehouse on Tobacco Row and was used for Union officers beginning in 1861. A lack of sanitation and overcrowding attributed to a high death rate among prisoners.

[62] Moyamensing Prison; a Gothic designed prison built in 1832, located on a neck of land between Passyunk and Wicaco at 10th and Reed streets in South Philadelphia. The cells were 9' by 14" and the prison once held the notorious H.H. Holmes (Herman Webster Mudgett) and the Abolitionist Passmore Williamson. The building was designed by Thomas Ustick Walter.

[63] William H. Walter had his portrait taken at this establishment on his return from service. This portrait is still in family possession.

www.ingramcontent.com/pod-product-compliance
Lightning Source LLC
Chambersburg PA
CBHW080248170426
43192CB00014BA/2601